"The world today needs more changemakers. people but her book can help any educator d roadmap to better instruction along with being a guide to how we and our students can all be more empathic while tackling the challenges that will truly change our world. Jennifer is an inspiration and this book is nothing less than inspirational."

STEVEN W. ANDERSON

Digital Learning and Relationship Evangelist, @web20classroom

"Jennifer Williams is the teacher we all wish we had in school, equally knowledgeable and talented as she is caring and empathetic. Like all the best teachers, Jennifer fully appreciates that educating the next generation can't just be about reading, writing, or even STEAM. Rather, it is about pushing students to dream big, holding their hands as they find their voices, helping them discover passion and purpose, encouraging them to be bold and demand action, and ensuring that they believe in the power they possess. This should be easier than ever before: edtech shines in removing classroom walls, democratizing creation and communication, showcasing diverse cultures, ideas, values, and opinions, making the big world of ours feel a bit more intimate, and amplifying even the smallest of voices. We have the tools, we just need an experienced guide encouraging us to use them. In this wonderful book Jennifer takes us educators on a journey, helping us discover how the tools at our disposal can empower us, and our students, to find our voices and passions and make a difference. *Teach Boldly* is an inspiring and much-needed read. Thank you, Jennifer!"

BEN FORTA

Author, Educator, and Adobe Sr. Dir. of Education Initiatives

"*Teach Boldly* by Dr. Jennifer Williams is more than just a one-stop read. It is an entry point into a engaging conversation that is meant to inspire others to change the world. Jen invites you to tap into your passions to compel positive change on the classroom, schoolhouse, and global level. Reading *Teach Boldly* is an invitational journey for all educators and students to take purposeful, giant steps to make our world a better place. Jen's words will call for repeated visits to *Teach Boldly* to engage with her profiles in peacemaker courage and intentional classroom resources. As I read this beautifully composed tome, I could hear the sincerity and compassion in Jen's voice. *Teach Boldly* is not only a book that stands as an inspiring call to action, but it resonates as a classic must-read professional book which stands the test of time."

SEAN GAILLARD

Principal, Founder of #CelebrateMonday, and Author of *The Pepper Effect*

"Dr. Williams' book *Teach Boldly* is a refreshing guidebook, toolkit, and journal for any educator who is committed to teaching for global citizenship in exciting, relevant, and technology-infused ways! At first glance, the book provides an exhaustive list of tech tools (and pedagogically sound ideas for implementing them!) that can serve as grab-and-go activities for any teacher; but Dr. Williams also provides, through direct prompts as well as through her own candid reflections on practice and learning, abundant space for educators to contemplate the intersections of pedagogy and educational frameworks with theories of social good, leadership, and social and ecological justice. *Teach Boldly* models creativity, reflection, and bold commitment to social good in a way that both challenges and empowers all teachers to see their classrooms, libraries, and buildings as openings for collaboration and leadership around building sustainable good in our world."

MATT HAMILTON

High School Teacher, @mhamiltonedu

"Jennifer Williams and the #TeachSDGs network are helping the young leaders of tomorrow see how the issues they care about in their communities resonate on a global scale. *Teach Boldly* is full of practical tools to help educators spark the passion and purpose of the young into positive action."

RAJESH MIRCHANDANI
Chief Communications Officer, United Nations Foundation

"Jennifer Williams, a consummate connected educator, invites you on a journey to help discover the value of social good in education and in doing so, introduces you to amazing educators from around the world and their practices. If you believe that your students should be adding value and doing good in the world, then this book is a great starting point for you!"

MEENOO RAMI
Author, *Thrive: 5 Ways to (Re)Invigorate Your Teaching*

"In a world where technology is advancing at an exponential rate and our children are craving the opportunity to shape the planet they will inherit from us, Dr. Jennifer Williams lays out a beautiful, practical vision of how we can empower the next generation to take action in shaping our global community. *Teach Boldly* balances big ideas about education with authentic examples of how educators can make learning meaningful for students. It is a must-read for anyone who believes education is the key to a bright future."

MICHAEL SOSKIL
2017-2018 Pennsylvania Teacher of the Year and Co-Author of
Teaching in the Fourth Industrial Revolution

"*Teach Boldly* is a stand-out resource! It's a must-read for anyone interested in a new paradigm of learning that focuses on real-world, learner-driven, social good learning experiences supported by the powerful technologies already at the fingertips of our learners. It's all here—a roadmap for your journey to designing your own classroom of impact. From establishing purpose to carving out time and designing learning spaces, Jen has included personal stories and robust examples to inspire you to transform your learners into curious thinkers ready to make a difference in the world and their communities. Are you ready to embrace the challenge to use edtech for social good? Your journey starts today with *Teach Boldly*!"

RANDY ZIEGENFUSS, Ed.D.
Superintendent, Salisbury Township School District

TEACH BOLDLY

USING EDTECH
FOR SOCIAL GOOD

JENNIFER WILLIAMS

International Society for Technology in Education

PORTLAND, OREGON • ARLINGTON, VA

Teach Boldly
USING EDTECH FOR SOCIAL GOOD

Jennifer Williams

Acquisitions Editor: Valerie Witte
Editor: Stephanie Argy
Copy Editor: Lisa Hein
Proofreader: Ernesto Yermoli
Indexer: Valerie Haynes Perry
Book Design and Production: Danielle Foster
Cover Design: Edwin Ouellette

Library of Congress Cataloging-in-Publication Data Available

First Edition

ISBN: 978-1-56484-794-2

Ebook version available

Printed in the United States of America

ABOUT ISTE

The International Society for Technology in Education (ISTE) is a nonprofit organization that works with the global education community to accelerate the use of technology to solve tough problems and inspire innovation. Our worldwide network believes in the potential technology holds to transform teaching and learning.

ISTE sets a bold vision for education transformation through the ISTE Standards, a framework for students, educators, administrators, coaches and computer science educators to rethink education and create innovative learning environments. ISTE hosts the annual ISTE Conference & Expo, one of the world's most influential edtech events. The organization's professional learning offerings include online courses, professional networks, year-round academies, peer-reviewed journals and other publications. ISTE is also the leading publisher of books focused on technology in education. For more information or to become an ISTE member, visit iste.org. Subscribe to ISTE's YouTube channel and connect with ISTE on Twitter, Facebook and LinkedIn.

RELATED ISTE TITLES

To see all books available from ISTE, please visit iste.org/resources.

ABOUT THE AUTHOR

 Recognized as a transformational leader in education, Jennifer Williams has dedicated herself to the field of education for more than twenty years through her roles as a professor, school administrator, literacy specialist, and classroom teacher. In her current work as the co-founder and executive director for the nonprofit organization Take Action Global (@TakeActionEdu), Jennifer helps to build schools in refugee camps and in remote areas of Africa, Asia, and South America, and she supports global school programs to empower students and teachers to take action on social good. In addition, she is the co-founder of TeachSDGs, the United Nations—appointed organization that has connected more than 30,000 international educators to the Sustainable Development Goals. She is a professor at Saint Leo University in both the College of Education and the College of Graduate Education, and she champions teachers, preservice teachers, and students to prepare for their futures in a world that will prioritize ingenuity, innovation, and exploration. Jennifer writes for *Edutopia*, *Education Week*, and the International Literacy Association, and she is the co-founder of Edcamp Tampa Bay and Edcamp Literacy. She is a Microsoft Innovative Educator Expert, a Kahoot! Founding Ambassador, a Nearpod PioNear, and a Squirrels Alpha Squirrel. In 2016 Jennifer was number 33 on Onalytica's list of the 200 Top Education Influencers, and in 2017 she was one of Onalytica's top women edtech influencers based on her work in education and educational technology. Jennifer is inspired every day by teachers and students who are catalysts for making the world a better place!

IN APPRECIATION

It is with deep appreciation that I acknowledge the people who have supported me with a lifetime of experiences that led me to this moment—the realization of my childhood dream to become an author.

Grateful to be surrounded by love:

To my high-school sweetheart and partner in life, Todd, thank you for always making me feel that my biggest hopes and dreams are exactly the ones I should go after, and at full speed. Thank you for creating time and space for me to write this book and always supporting me to "get to it!" To our children, Wyatt, Owen, and Grace, thank you for giving me the greatest gift of being your mother. Your faces and smiles are the most beautiful things my eyes have ever seen. You all are my heart and my home and my happiness. (Murphy and Fig, too!)

To my mom and dad, thank you for teaching me to seek out adventure, live with integrity, stand up for those in need, and believe in the power of love and family. Thank you for always believing in me and loving me. To my sister, Heather, thank you for being my best friend and for cheering me on. You have wrapped your arms around my dreams and aspirations in life and lifted them up. I am by your side always.

To my entire family—my nieces and grandparents, aunts and cousins, and friends who have been part of my family—thank you for making me who I am today and for loving me.

Grateful to be surrounded by artistic expression and humanity:

To the many people along the way who have shown me the power of creative expression, I am thankful. I offer praise to the writers who inspired me as a young girl and who showed me that the written word has the power to change lives; thank you, Anne Frank, T.S. Eliot, Elie Wiesel, Astrid Lindgren, E.B. White, Maurice Sendak, Louisa May Alcott, Louis Sachar, Richard Scarry, and Frances Hodgson Burnett.

I feel grateful to have been inspired during my many months of writing this book by listening to the songs of The Lumineers, Digable Planets, The Beatles, and Vitamin String Quartet and by surrounding myself with the art of Joan Miró, Christopher Still, Shepard Fairey, Carlton Ward Jr, my grandmother Bea Roberts, and my children Wyatt, Owen, and Grace.

Grateful to be surrounded by support and inspiration:

Appreciation and praise to the entire team at ISTE for believing in this project and for prioritizing social good, equity, and student action in education and in edtech. Deepest gratitude to my editors Stephanie Argy and Valerie Witte for constant support, kind words, and encouragement (every hour of every day— I knew you were there with me through it all). Many thanks to the copy editors, designers, reviewers, researchers, and endorsers—all who were involved in the design and production of this book.

I offer my appreciation and praise to my colleagues—educators around the globe who work each and every day to spark positive change in our world through education. I am grateful for my own teachers from preschool through university, my colleagues who taught in classrooms next door to mine and in classrooms in different parts of our world, and all TeachSDGs educators and PLN friends from Twitter and Instagram. I am thankful for Maria Montessori, Jane Goodall, and Sara Lawrence-Lightfoot, who, as pioneers in education and social good, have helped to shape my views of teaching, learning, and humanity.

Grateful for the shared stories of global peacemakers in education who embody ingenuity, persistence, change, and kindness:

FEATURED EDUCATORS IN SPOTLIGHTS AND PORTRAITS:

- Andrew Arevalo
- Alison Bellwood
- Juli-Anne Benjamin
- Don Buckley
- Jessica Burnquist
- Monica Burns
- Ayush Chopra
- Melissa Collins
- Mike Crowley
- Michael Dunlea
- Mary Jeanne Farris
- Laura Fleming
- Sean Gaillard
- Noah Garcia-Hassell
- Loise Gichuhi
- Kristin Harrington
- Michael Hernandez
- Steve Isaacs
- Oluwaseun Kayode

- Craig Kemp
- Hope Kennedy
- Kathi Kersznowski
- Yau-Jau Ku
- Danish Kurani
- Andrew Marcinek
- Amber McCormick
- Ada McKim
- Estella Owoimaha-Church
- Rob Paul
- Stephen Peters
- Billy Spicer
- Jacob Sule
- Koen Timmers
- Wendy Turner
- Olivia Van Ledtje
- Cleary Vaughan-Lee
- David Willows
- Claudio Zavala, Jr.

FEATURED STUDENT ARTISTS WITH SUBMITTING TEACHERS:

- Owen Dunno (grade 8) and teacher Luisa Vargas

- Marigold Mioc (age 9) and program Global Oneness Project and HundrED

- Max Yang (grade 8) and teacher Donna Guerin

- Ellie Buis (grade 1)

- Kaitlyn Zong (grade 11) and teacher Aaron Yetter, principal Heather Morningstar, and superintendent Randy Ziegenfuss

- Lee Patel (grade 12) and teacher Estella Owoimaha-Church

- Grace Williams (grade 4)

Grateful to be surrounded by young voices of hope:

To peacemakers Anne Frank, Ruby Bridges, and Ryan White, who were some of my earliest models of strength, compassion, perseverance, and social good, thank you for teaching me that the voices of children and youth deserve to be heard. I offer my deepest appreciation and praise and honor your work and your lives.

To all my students, thank you for the lessons you taught me. And to all the children of the world, you are our greatest hope.

DEDICATION

For Todd, my sweet love, and Wyatt, Owen, and Grace, our beautiful children— you are my world, my happiness, my purpose.

In memory of my grandmother, Bea Roberts, who showed me the importance of being curious as an explorer, questioner, and dreamer.

"I'll make my voice heard, I'll go out into the world and work for mankind."

—*Anne Frank, April 11, 1944*

CONTENTS

1   BE PART OF SOMETHING BIGGER THAN ONESELF   1

2 THE TIME YOU GIVE TO THE THINGS YOU VALUE   37

3 THE HUMAN-CENTERED LEARNING ENVIRONMENT 67

4 SHARING STORIES TO OFFER PANORAMA 99

5 CONSCIOUS CONSUMERS: ADDING CONTEXT TO THE TOOL 127

6 I'D LIKE TO TEACH THE WORLD TO _____. 145

LETTER TO READERS
By Olivia Van Ledtje, Student Activist

Dear Readers,

I am soooooooo excited to welcome you to *Teach Boldly: Using Edtech for Social Good* by my friend and mentor, Jennifer Williams. I bet you're here reading this book because you love the world as much as me! And guess what? This book will take you on an incredible reading and thinking adventure! You'll meet inspiring people doing amazing work for the world, and most especially, get ideas to help kids like me!

I hope as you read Jennifer's words, you'll consider the beautiful invitation she gives you to think about students as the center of your work. I promise that center will be a giant heartbeep in your teaching life! Jennifer calls kids like me PeaceMAKERS—and this book encourages you to create a wave of action for PeaceMAKERS everywhere.

As a book activist, I am so inspired by how authors use words. So, I invite you with my own special mashup poem, influenced by my absolute favorite Silly WordMAKER poet, Shel Silverstein:

> *If you're a dreamer, a wisher, a lover of words!*
> *Come in!*
> *If you're a maker, a believer, a lover of the world!*
> *Come in!*
> *If you're a techie, a seeker, and hoper for social good!*
> *Come in! Come in!*

Sincerely, Your PeaceMAKER and Silly WordMAKER,

Olivia Van Ledtje

INTRODUCTION

I ALWAYS KNEW I WOULD BE A TEACHER. As a young child, I would play imaginary school, and from the head of my bed, I would look out onto imaginary students sitting in rows of imaginary desks. The "classroom" was confined by the space of my bed, so I only had room for approximately ten "students." In my mind as that young child, those students likely looked like me, had names like children I knew, and enjoyed the same stories and activities I had come to love.

I would take attendance and call out their names. If any of my imaginary students were absent, I would wonder if they had a dentist appointment, or maybe a slight cold that was keeping them home to rest up. I read them stories from my own bookshelf—paperback and hardback books with characters who mostly looked and lived like me. I made worksheets with math problems, gave them imaginary tests, and recorded grades in my handmade gradebook; I moved their invisible desks if they were too chatty; I gave them paper certificates I made with love for their efforts and their good performance. All was well in my imaginary classroom.

As the students' imaginary teacher, I felt happy when they got imaginary As. I knew they were happy and didn't worry about their futures. In fact, I didn't give much thought to my imaginary students' futures or to mine but simply envisioned the future as a world that looked very similar to the one I was living in—a simple life with dinners at 6 p.m., homework, bedtime, and school the next day.

What I had right was that I always knew I wanted to be a teacher. Everything else in those daydreams of teaching, I pretty much had wrong.

Years later, as I entered my first classroom, I quickly found that real life as an educator was very different from the made-up teaching world I had created in my mind. My students' stories were in the most amazing ways so very different from my own. I learned about their dreams, their fears, their passions, and the challenges life had delivered to them.

Everything I had planned for—making nice little certificates for good attendance or being worried only about moving students for talking a little too much—was not part of my real-life job description.

As a teacher, I understood that structures for balance, curiosity, creativity, kindness, and peace are informed by our earliest life experiences, so my job description expanded to the development and support of skills that could help students share their stories and prepare for their futures. And, as I learned more about what teaching and learning looked like in my own classroom, I found that teaching, learning, school, and the future did not have one single definition.

With students in my classroom from countries other than my own in the U.S., I became interested in what school looked like on different parts of our planet.

One of the first global educators I met was Loise Gichuhi, a professor from Nairobi, Kenya. We shared stories online and compared what school looked like from each of our perspectives. She shared with me that students in the neighboring rural communities did not have books. Interested in learning more, I asked her to share a photo of one of the schools.

In a photo Loise shared, I was amazed to see how narrow my definition of school had been. The school in the photo she sent me did not have desks or math worksheets or even a building. It was instead an outdoor space for students with a blackboard propped against an old crooked tree. Regrettably, my first emotion in seeing this image was sadness. How would learning look for these students? But then I heard that for these children, school was their source of food as well as education. Students would walk long distances to come and be nourished and to gain new knowledge. School equaled hope and community and life.

0.1 Community
School in Nairobi

After Loise taught me about the power of school in Nairobi, I became increasingly interested in education on a global level. I started to ask, "What does learning look like in our world of classrooms?" and set out to visit schools outside of the U.S. to learn more. I soon found that school as we know it, informed by tradition and influenced by innovation, is changing everywhere.

Through Twitter and videoconferencing tools such as Skype, I have since connected with thousands of teachers and classrooms globally. I have met teachers who create change where it may not exist, who find solutions when paths are not clear, and who set out with their students to MAKE the world in which they hope to live. I call these teachers, who inspire my work each day, my PeaceMAKERS.

As we move into a future that will advance just as we learn it, we need to be adaptable, and we need to learn with and from the experiences of others. We are at an incredibly exciting but also pivotal point in education. As educators—whether we knew early on that we were destined to teach or discovered the importance of joining this noble profession of education later in life—we all have an opportunity to make a difference as PeaceMAKERS. With innovation and technology supporting us as we go, it is our time to lay out paths for people and the planet with our students. I encourage all teachers of the world to be curious and bold, and I offer this book, *Teach Boldly: Using Edtech for Social Good*, to support you in your efforts to reimagine what it means to be a teacher and to make your special mark on our world.

WHAT THIS BOOK AIMS TO DO

Rather than being passive participants in society, today's students are ready to design, dream, and MAKE the future! This book is offered as a practical guide for educators who want to activate positive change in teaching and learning through bold, innovative practices, meaningful uses of technology, and collaborations with diverse populations of people locally and globally. With inspiration from stories of real-world PeaceMAKERS in education, readers are invited to be active participants in the reading experience and to create ready-to-go action plans for themselves as educators, for their classroom communities, and for global communities.

Through a humanistic lens of social good, this book is offered with a strong belief in the prioritization of people—their passions, their perspectives, and the great power they have to positively impact the world. In an effort to model equity and access to learning, this book offers practical and actionable ideas that can be used by all and for all.

My hope is that this book will spark conversation and action on social good— among students, colleagues, and communities. It aims to:

- Offer a reading experience based on new insights and current practices in the area of innovation and instructional design, with practical ideas for connecting students at local and global levels through a shared goal of promoting social good and positive change.

xx

- Support teachers as they celebrate diversity, cultivate empathy, and promote expression of ideas with students as global collaborators and also as empowered learners, digital citizens, knowledge constructors, innovative designers, computational thinkers, and creative communicators.

- Provide a plan for building routines and rituals through partnerships and agency. Instead of proclaiming a narrow prescription or proposing a project that could be viewed as an "add-on" to curricula, this book offers educators practical ideas that can be integrated into everyday practices and into the culture of a classroom to prioritize global perspectives and social good in all parts of the school day.

This book should not be your only source of information, and throughout its pages you will find information about additional sources of expertise and alternative views.

PRESENCE, PURPOSE, AND PERSPECTIVE

PRESENCE: This book is an invitation to be present.

This book as a practical guide invites you as a reader to pause and reflect on current practices and on intended practices. I seek to leave buzzwords and jargon behind, and to meet you where you are with respect to experience, resources, mindsets, and intentions. With a commitment to inviting all teachers to work in solidarity for the good of all, I affirm to be present with you in taking action on creating positive change for students, for educators, and for the world.

PURPOSE: This book is an invitation to pull purpose to the center.

My intention with this book is to provide an inclusive and welcoming space that is focused on action and on purpose. The text of the book, the reader, and the interaction between the reader and the text are all seen as essential components to the process of making meaning. You as the reader are invited to be an active constructor of knowledge in the reading and learning experience. In writing this book, I join the interaction with the assumption that readers come with a desire to seek new learning and practices, so my purpose is to offer readers pathways for success—void of barriers or prohibitive walls—that allow for access and meaningful points of entry.

PERSPECTIVE: This book is an invitation to lean into perspective.

I consciously enter into this book with a recognition that my perspective is limited to one singular life experience. This book is offered with an appreciation that readers enter into the reading experience with unique and varied backgrounds, experiences, beliefs, and values. In an effort to highlight that there is not one universal experience or one singular story, I aim to recognize bias and to spotlight stories from as many diverse perspectives as possible. Though many people contributed by sharing their stories, ideas, and viewpoints, I understand that there are still many more voices that need to be included. It is my hope that this book is just the beginning of the conversation and that we can continue to find ways to come together, to talk, and to celebrate the richness, complexity, and beauty of our shared human experience.

STRUCTURE OF THE BOOK

This book is organized into six core chapters, each of which offers examples from classrooms, ideas for instruction, explanations of innovations in pedagogy and technology, and the opportunity to create a customized take-action plan for your work.

Key Chapter Elements

Inspirational Stories

Each of the six chapters begins with a personal or inspirational story intended to connect with the heart and the mind. As you journey through these pages, I encourage you to find connections and sources of inspiration from your own life and experiences.

Take ACTION

Take ACTION ideas are presented in each chapter to help you as an educator act on new learning. Take ACTION ideas allow readers to synthesize, prioritize, and apply approaches to their current practice.

BOLD Invitation

Each chapter presents one "dream big, do big" idea in the form of a BOLD Invitation. Readers can choose to accept these invitations or can bookmark and revisit them later.

My PeaceMAKER Profile

This book is designed to be an interactive reading experience, and the My PeaceMAKER Profile exercise invites you to build a portfolio of your learning. The profile allows you to document your journey and demonstrate new learning, points of action, and reflection. The profile can be shared as part of professional learning plans or collaborative learning activities. Each chapter includes a guided PeaceMAKER Profile activity that relates to the topic of that chapter. Together, all six activities represent the My PeaceMAKER Profile, which is also available at jenwilliamsedu.com/peacemaker-profile.html.

Portrait of a PeaceMAKER Vignettes

The book also contains three Portrait of a PeaceMAKER vignettes, which provide views into the work, the intentions, and the lives of educators who are dedicated to making a difference in schools and in society. These portraits allow us to better understand what drives people and their decisions when they teach boldly and use edtech for social good. Additionally, three exemplars of edtech programs committed to social good are offered in Appendix C.

ISTE Standards for Educators and Students

The International Society for Technology in Education (ISTE) as an organization is committed to serving and supporting global educators as they use technology to transform teaching and learning, accelerate innovation, and solve the tough problems we face in education. The ISTE Standards are offered as frameworks to help educators and education leaders reengineer schools and classrooms for digital age learning (ISTE, 2019). Frameworks (available at iste.org/standards) are available for students, educators, education leaders, coaches, and computer science educators. In this book, ideas shared in chapters directly correlate to ISTE Standards for Educators and ISTE Standards for Students; the relevant standards are show below, in **figures 0.2** and **0.3**. The Standards appear in full in Appendix A (Educators) and Appendix B (Students).

	1 Learner	2 Leader	3 Citizen	4 Collaborator	5 Designer	6 Facilitator	7 Analyst
Ch 1			3a, 3b	4c	5b	6a, 6c, 6d	
Ch 2	1a	2a	3a		5b	6a	
Ch 3	1b, 1c, 1d			4c		6b, 6c, 6d	
Ch 4	1b, 1c	2a, 2b, 2c	3a, 3b, 3c, 3d	4a, 4b, 4c, 4d	5a, 5b, 5c	6a, 6b, 6c, 6d	7a, 7b, 7c
Ch 5	1a	2c	3b	4b	5a		7b
Ch 6	1a, 1b, 1c	2a, 2b, 2c	3d	4a, 4b, 4c, 4d			

0.2 ISTE Standards for Educators by Chapter

	1 Empowered Student	2 Digital Citizen	3 Knowledge Constructor	4 Innovative Designer	5 Computational Thinker	6 Creative Communicator	7 Global Collaborator
Ch 1	1b	2a, 2b, 2c	3a, 3b, 3c, 3d	4a, 4b, 4c, 4d			7d
Ch 2	1a			4a, 4b		6b, 6c, 6d	7a
Ch 3		2b			5a, 5c	6b, 6d	
Ch 4	1c, 1d	2a, 2b, 2c, 2d	3a, 3b, 3c, 3d			6a, 6b, 6c, 6d	7a, 7b, 7c, 7d
Ch 5	1d	2d				6a	
Ch 6							

0.3 ISTE Standards for Students by Chapter

WAYS TO CONNECT

Get Social!

Social learning is powerful learning. It is shared, it is responsive, it is developed over time and through experience. You are invited to join the global conversation on social media with the hashtags #TeachBoldly and #socialgood. Throughout the book, I note contributors with their Twitter handles. Be sure to connect with them and share your ideas and feedback. We are all better when we are learning together.

My Website

Templates, discussions, and new resources are available on my website at JenWilliamsEdu.com. And you can always reach out to me on Twitter at @JenWilliamsEdu.

School-Wide Learning Experiences for Social Good

Schools and networks of educators can engage with this book and the My PeaceMAKER Profile experience as groups. Ideas for book clubs, Twitter chats, and Professional Learning Communities (PLCs) are offered in Appendix D.

MY HOPE FOR YOU

Reading is an experience.

Reading is learning and sharing.

Reading is an action.

Reading is questioning.

Every reader of this book is beautifully unique. It is my hope for you that your experience reading and interacting with this book is unlike anyone else's. I am hopeful you will expand these ideas to make them meaningful in your environment and your world.

I wrote this book with you as a teacher in my mind. I envision you—the teacher—as someone seeking a better way for the students you serve, whether you're in Texas, Hong Kong, Tanzania, or somewhere else; in a well-resourced classroom or in a space that only has tables and maybe not even enough chairs. Just as I view all the students of the world as my own, I view you as my colleague. I thank you for entering into this reading experience with me—and into this profession. I am ready to change the world with you!

Jen

With INNOVATION and technology

supporting us as we go,

it is our time to lay out paths

for people and the planet

with our students.

1

BE PART OF SOMETHING BIGGER THAN ONESELF

As teachers and students embark on their journey to do good in society, they must understand their purpose and the means by which they can bring change. This chapter introduces human rights goals and frameworks that can offer them inspiration, as well as design thinking principles that can help them devise and implement actions.

Spearmint by Owen Dunno, Grade 8
Teacher: Luisa Vargas, Director of Art Education
Christ Episcopal School, Rockville, MD, USA

Inspiration: Power of a Teacher's Presence

The quick brown fox jumps over the lazy dog.

Etched in my mind is the memory of this sentence, written in dusty white chalk on our classroom blackboard. Had it been a different class from a different year of my schooling, I might have said "a blackboard *in the front of the room*," but this classroom was unlike others I had known. Our fourth-grade teacher, Mrs. Buttery, had purposefully arranged our individual desks into one large open rectangle, so the room never had a front or a back or a "good seat" or a "not-so-good one." I imagine we were known by other teachers as quite the chatty group, but Mrs. Buttery loved us just the way we were. She welcomed our conversations and laughed and dreamed right along with us. I can still picture her as she walked around the perimeter of our room, always moving and always smiling. Each day she wore long, flowing skirts that would nearly touch the floor, which gave me the illusion she was almost floating.

This day, she directed our attention to the sentence: "The quick brown fox jumps over the lazy dog." Our task was to uncover what was special about the sentence, and we were to solve this puzzle through an inspired process of inquiry and exploration. Our classroom was alive with ideas. As to be expected from the literal minds of nine- and ten-year-old children, we narrowed in on the nouns and on possible explanations for why this dog was so lazy and what might be causing this fox to be filled with such energy. Through Mrs. Buttery's scaffolded questions and gentle guidance, we finally found what made this sentence so special and unique—the letters. All letters of our English alphabet represented. In one sentence! For me, a child who loved words and letters as if they were my friends, this was magical.

That lesson was one of many from that year in Mrs. Buttery's class that would stick with me. Each day that we entered her classroom—our classroom—we knew she would share a new adventure with us. With stories of distant cultures and maps of lands old and new, she opened up a world beyond our chatty little class on the Gulf Coast of Florida.

Later that same year, I learned of Africa. This wasn't the type of learning I had experienced before, where Africa was an item in a memorized list of continents. By that point, I had lists and lists of information I had learned by rote: planets and state capitals and food groups. This new type of learning brought me to a place of wanting not just to learn, but to *know*. Noticing this new interest of mine, Mrs. Buttery brought me books and newspaper clippings, and I soon came to understand the incredible challenges faced by many African children.

It never occurred to me that I was learning *about* the struggles of the people of Africa; in my mind I was learning *with* them. How could a child like me—just born in a different place on our planet—be without schools that had books and blackboards and, even more troubling, without access to medication and water and food? Doorways that led to teachers who invited wonder and discovery were not part of many of these children's days. And so, with a teacher who told me to keep going and parents who always inspired me to think bigger than myself, I set out to do anything I could. I told anyone who would listen about the conditions for children in these certain parts of Africa at the time (this was during the 1985 Ethiopian famine), and I worked to collect as many coin and dollar donations as I possibly could. After months of collecting money and a constant play-rewind-repeat of "We Are the World" (my self-selected theme song), I delivered my little (but big to me) $300 of funds raised to the Red Cross.

Today, looking back, I can see the signpost moments in my life and the way my experiences in education shaped me as an educator—and as a person. With teachers like Mrs. Buttery who were fully present, who inspired and empowered our ideas as students, and who offered us spaces to explore new worlds beyond our own with the best technologies and resources available at the time, education opened up pathways to let each of us mold and design our own futures. Since those days in 1985, my journey has been dedicated to seeking quality education for all. I have found my community of other globally minded educators who, like me, see all the world's children as their own.

Positioning students as knowledge constructors and empowered, creative communicators enables us as teachers to help foster the passions and dreams of all our students. We don't just open doorways, we build them.

Through technology-infused practices that allow for design, collaboration, and digital citizenship in learning, I believe that educators of the world, present in this moment of teaching and learning, can come together in solidarity to help rewrite the "stories of possible" in our global communities, so that students can move beyond concerns about seeking out quality learning or meals or water, and instead can explore puzzles of energetic foxes and lazy dogs and dream with chatty classmates about stories that seem filled with wonder and magic. I have hope.

SOCIAL GOOD IN EDUCATION

In classrooms and in schools, teachers and students are coming together to take action on creating change. Technology for social good makes it possible to share diverse perspectives, values, and beliefs. It allows for engagement through collaborative activities and coordination of efforts for increased impact. Social good provides purpose for inquiry-driven practices and project-based learning (PBL) by giving students the opportunity to engage in work that is relevant, interesting, and connected to the human experience. Though dedicated efforts for social good are relatively new in K—12 education, students and teachers are seeing how and where their voices fit in the global conversation, and that they are needed.

Traditionally, work around social good has been mostly reserved for the profession of social work. Programs, services, and products would target areas of need to promote well-being and to support causes in areas such as human rights, immigration, the environment, poverty, and access to housing, food, and clean water. In recent years, however, work around social good has spread into other professional sectors such as business, technology, and social entrepreneurship. With a sense of urgency and purpose, people from all areas of life, in all parts of the world, and of all ages are responding through committed grassroots efforts. Those of us in education are finding that innovative methods of awareness, advocacy, and activism are enabling us to make a positive difference for our world.

CONCEPTUAL MODEL OF SOCIAL GOOD

"Social good refers to services or products that promote human well-being on a large scale" (Mor Barak, 2018, p. 762). Three anchor themes that serve as a conceptual model for social good and describe the universal elements for the work within social good include (a) environmental justice and sustainability, (b) social inclusion, and (c) peace, harmony, and collaboration (Mor Barak, 2018).

These themes, fitting in at all grade levels and across all content areas within K—12 education, provide logical pathways for educators ready to support students in social-good efforts.

OUR ROLE IN TEACHING SOCIAL GOOD

What are our roles as educators in spaces of social good and social change? The job of a teacher involves developing skills in areas such as reading, writing, math, science, and history, but how do competencies such as kindness, empathy, commitment to action, and resilience fit in?

In considering this question, the phrase "raising our children" comes to mind. I use this phrase often—as a mother of three, as a teacher, and even in writing hopeful sentences such as, "As teachers, we must help raise children to reach their full potentials." The verb "raise" has a powerful meaning: "to lift up, to move to a higher position or level." In our work as teachers, we are in fact raising the children in our care. We hold them up and give them the right amount of boost when needed.

As my teacher Mrs. Buttery did for me, we can help shape the experiences of our students by meeting them with curiosity and interest. By endorsing a general trajectory while leaving room for exploration and wonder, we can invite our students to connect to their passions and to discover possibilities that may ultimately change their paths in life. But it takes discipline on our part to use our power as educators responsibly.

To "teach boldly" may mean that we take action, or it may mean that we simply listen without judgment. To build a culture grounded in inquiry and discourse, we need to guide our students so that they build on questions, seek out experts, and become confident individuals who are comfortable with imperfection and change. As teachers, we raise these children; we help them to chart their own visions for a better world and to establish the way they hope to contribute.

COLLECTIVE POWER TO CHANGE THE WORLD

Nil neart gancur le cheile. Translated from Irish to English, this means "There is no strength without unity." Bernadette Dwyer (@dwyerbe) of Ireland, one of my friends and mentors, shared this phrase with me when emphasizing the power of people coming together for progress.

For adults, moments of mindset change may not come easily or often, but as educators we witness this in children every day. We see those little "aha" moments, when students pause, readjust, and move forward. And in those moments, we know that life for them, in a tiny way, will be changed forever. All those little flashes of awareness and understanding ultimately can combine to create a society anchored in kindness, empathy, and inclusivity.

By using edtech for social good, we can collectively drive change. Work in this area can take many forms: students creating campaigns, advocating for causes, or taking dedicated actions as activists for change. There are subtle differences in terminology and in scope, but all serve as options for taking action for social good in education.

Campaigning

Students passionate about a school or local initiative can create campaigns. These might take the form of a schoolwide book drive for literacy efforts or a class program for recycling. Campaigning gives students of all ages a way to take action and give back to their own community.

Advocacy

Students involved in advocacy work take action on behalf of another person, group, or cause. They often combine their efforts with those of a larger group of people and look to the leaders of that group for direction, organization, or specific actions. Service-learning projects often encourage advocacy- and awareness-building activities in addition to the service. Examples might include students joining efforts to provide a community with access to clean water or students joining a project to help animals in need of protection.

Activism

Student activism is typically associated with students taking intentional action to lead efforts with a specific goal of creating change, often in areas such as social justice, politics, or the environment. Activists take a position on an issue that is personally meaningful to them and offer a strong stance of support or dissent on a debatable topic. Means of activism by students most recently have included social media campaigns, marches, and the use of outreach, including blogging, podcasting, television interviews, and professional speaking.

In this work today, students are leading the way. A new generation of activists and global changemakers is engaging with radical kindness and having an impact on the international dialogue on societal issues and policy. Through the use of networks and compelling messages of solidarity and resilience, these activists are taking causes beyond the classroom to social media, city streets, and the steps of government buildings. By taking control of the story of their world and the one they want for their futures, they are attracting like-minded individuals and together changing the narrative surrounding issues that matter to them. These young people, as citizens of the world, are demonstrating that an individual person can make a positive impact on society. They are mighty and fearless and serve as voices of hope; the whole world is watching them.

March for Our Lives

March for Our Lives is a student-led activist movement dedicated to ending gun violence. Developed by Florida students from Marjory Stoneman Douglas High School who were seeking justice and action following the tragic shooting at their school in February 2018, the organization showed the world that student voice is strong and deserves to be heard. Through use of social media and televised town hall gatherings, and by assembling students across the country in voter registration events, the young activists spread their message far and wide. The March for Our Lives demonstrations held on March 24, 2018, were the beginning of their work to mobilize on gun control; more than 1.2 million people took part in more than 450 marches all over the United States. Today, the students work to change policy, advocating for gun violence prevention and for voter registration. Follow the efforts of their movement at marchforourlives.com and on Twitter at @AMarch4OurLives.

Climate Strike

In August 2018, fifteen-year-old Greta Thunberg (@GretaThunberg), a Swedish student activist, decided to skip school on a Friday to strike outside the parliament building in Stockholm in an attempt to get action on climate change. Several months later, she spoke at TEDxStockholm (youtube.com/watch?v= H2QxFM9y0tY) and then at the World Economic Forum at Davos.

With her mission expressed on a handmade sign that read "Skolstrejk för klimatet" ("School Strike for the Climate") and in a hashtag (#fridaysforfuture), she marched every Friday leading up to a world march in March of 2019. The #ClimateStrike march in 2019 brought more than one million students to the streets of the world. In 2019, *Time* named Greta one of the world's twenty-five most influential leaders, and she was nominated for the Nobel Peace Prize. At the time of publication of this book, she still marched every Friday.

#KeepReading

Olivia Van Ledtje (@TheLivBits) is a student activist for literacy and digital citizenship for children and the creator of LivBits, a project she started when she was only eight years old. She shares short videos about reading and connecting with passions, and she talks to students and teachers about the importance of student voice and ensuring that children feel they belong. "Technology helps me amplify my voice. I'm able to connect and be encouraged in my LivBits work by people all over the world," Liv shared with me. You can check out Liv's story of using digital tools for good on her website (thelivbits.com) and through her blog, videos, and social media.

Here are Liv's top three tips for students to take action for social good:

1. Stay hopeful and follow people who inspire you to create more.

2. Notice other people's messages and encourage their work.

3. Remember that your story can inspire others to take the risk to share their own.

#SDGSforChildren

1.1 Activist Ayush Chopra posts videos inspired by the Sustainable Development Goals.

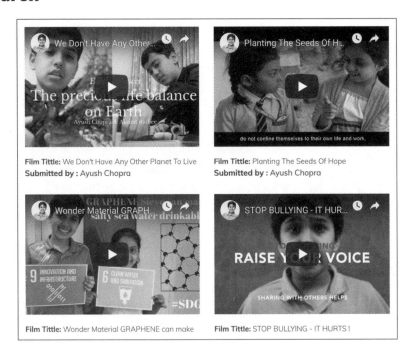

Film Tittle: We Don't Have Any Other Planet To Live
Submitted by : Ayush Chopra

Film Tittle: Planting The Seeds Of Hope
Submitted by : Ayush Chopra

Film Tittle: Wonder Material GRAPHENE can make

Film Tittle: STOP BULLYING - IT HURTS !

Ayush Chopra (@WizardAyush), known as Wizard Ayush by his peers and friends on social media, is a fifteen-year-old global activist working to create a safer and more sustainable future by empowering the voices of youth. He is the

Ariel Foundation International Youth Ambassador at the United Nations and is the founder of the SDGs for Children community (sdgsforchildren.org). In 2019, he published his first book, *Shaping a Fairer World with SDGs and Human Rights*, telling of his experiences with social transformation, and he shares weekly on his podcast and in YouTube videos. His efforts on human rights have been recognized with the 2019 Diana Award, and as the youngest ambassador to be invited to the Youth Human Rights International Summit at the United Nations in New York City, Ayush is set to continue to take action for good through activism and awareness efforts.

#FoodMilesMatter

1.2 Sixth-grade students at North Broward Preparatory School in Coconut Creek, Florida, created the Global Gardening Project and #FoodMilesMatter.

"We set out to reduce climate change and the excess emissions of fossil fuels by growing local food for our school cafeteria," the students of Food Miles Matter shared in 2019. Formed as a small group of sixth-grade students interested in creating a garden in their science class, the student team at Food Miles Matter moved swiftly from being campaigners to becoming activists. After seeing the benefits of their school garden and how it reduced the number of miles their food traveled from production to plate, they created the Global Gardening Project.

The students created videos and used their student-designed website (bit.ly /foodmilesmatter) and their student-run Twitter account (@FoodMilesMatter) to promote their work and connect with schools and experts. Each week, they meet with students in classrooms around the world to share their experiences and promote the message that food miles matter. In spring 2019, they were awarded $30,000 for their work when they won the Lexus Eco Challenge sponsored by Lexus and Scholastic. Through purpose and perseverance, they are making a difference in our world.

ESTABLISH PURPOSE

What might it look like to take action for social good in your classroom? Perhaps you and your students are interested in joining a global collaboration project. Maybe you want to create a project of your own. Or you might find that your students are interested in building an invention to solve a problem we are facing in the world. But before you decide what you want to do, you need to understand your "why" behind it all.

Take time to establish your purpose. This, I think, is the best lesson I have learned from working with students on social good and social action projects. Though it is tempting for educators to move students right into a cause ("Okay students, I would like you to pick something you care about and let's get going . . ."), the outcomes and impact will ultimately suffer. The difference between an exercise and an experience lies in the work you and your students do to establish purpose. The time spent in this phase is valuable and important.

Inspiration for Action

For us as educators, I have good news! There are two frameworks ideal for students seeking ways to connect to purpose:

1. The Universal Declaration of Human Rights

2. The Sustainable Development Goals

These are available to inspire lessons, help generate ideas for student projects, and drive change.

Universal Declaration of Human Rights

Adopted by the United Nations (UN) General Assembly on December 10, 1948, the Universal Declaration of Human Rights (UDHR) provided our world with a vision for protecting the rights of all humans. Organized and offered as a six-page document of thirty articles, it has been translated into more than 500 languages and is recognized by the Guinness Book of World Records as the most translated document in the world (GWR, 2009).

Students and teachers can visit the **UN website** (un.org/en/universal-declaration-human-rights) to access the document and translated versions, watch videos of people around the world reading the articles, read the illustrated version, read about the women who shaped the Universal Declaration, and listen to the famous 1948 audio clip, "The Declaration," in which Eleanor Roosevelt reads the preamble and all the articles.

Classrooms can also access and join in the conversation around the UDHR with the hashtags #RightsOutLoud and #StandUp4HumanRights.

The Sustainable Development Goals

In 2015, a document titled "Transforming Our World: The 2030 Agenda for Sustainable Development" laid out a plan to bring forth solutions to the most complex and urgent problems that we as global citizens are facing. The first line of the agenda's preamble, "This Agenda is a plan of action for people, planet, and prosperity," boldly frames a comprehensive road map for success and offers hope that the world will come together in common purpose to preserve and protect our futures.

This plan set forth by the United Nations identifies seventeen initiatives, known as the Sustainable Development Goals (SDGs or Global Goals) (**Figure 1.3**). Each of the goals—which range from eliminating poverty (Goal 1) to reducing inequalities (Goal 10) to climate action (Goal 13)—offers clear and measurable targets for countries and citizens to meet by the year 2030.

Students and teachers can learn more about the Global Goals by visiting sustainabledevelopment.un.org. There they can view goals by targets and indicators, by progress, and by related resources.

1.3 Teachers can use the UN's 17 Sustainable Development Goals to guide students toward purpose (UN, 2015).

Using the UDHR and SDGs to Connect to Purpose and Action

The UDHR and SDGs can be entry points into conversations about social good with students in the classroom. Here are a few simple ways you as an educator can gear up for the learning experience with students:

- Find a cause aligned to the UDHR or the SDGs and your own work. Contribute time or public support to causes and use the tag #RightsOutLoud and #TeachSDGs on social media.

- Consider ways to keep people and the planet at the center of all that you do. Invest in relationships and invite people who are representative of diverse perspectives or experiences into conversations and projects.

- Take action and stay informed. Follow @UN, @UNFoundation, and @TeachSDGs on Twitter, and download the SDGs in Action app (sdgsinaction.com) to get updates on the progress of the global goals.

- Print out the Global Goals poster or images of the individual goals (sustainabledevelopment.un.org/sdgs) and post them in your classroom. They're available in the six official languages of the UN: Arabic, Chinese, English, French, Russian, and Spanish. Find small ways to join forces and partner with others to take steps to reach these ambitious goals as part of a united and cooperative world.

- To work on investigations for extended periods of time, connect the UDHR and the SDGs to high quality Project Based Learning (HQPBL). Visit the HQPBL website (hqpbl.org) to download frameworks available in English and Spanish.

1.4 Students learn about the Global Goals.

WORLD'S LARGEST LESSON

DESIGN THINKING AND HUMAN-CENTERED DESIGN

In our efforts to help students develop as global citizens, we as educators are working to build student global competence. Global competency is defined as the "possession of knowledge, skills, and dispositions to understand and act creatively on issues of global significance" (Asia Society & OECD, 2018).

Design thinking and human-centered design (HCD) frameworks support development of global competence and efforts of social good. Though the terms are sometimes used interchangeably, there are distinctions between the two. Design thinking is an iterative problem-solving approach that consists of five phases: (1) emphasize, (2) define, (3) ideate, (4) prototype, and (5) test. Human-centered design is a form of design thinking organized into three phases: (1) inspiration, (2) ideation, and (3) implementation. Both frameworks prioritize creative problem solving, creativity and innovation, and the user and the problems he or she faces. Thus, design thinking and HCD frameworks provide instructional design structures that are complementary to the work of social good and social action in the classroom.

Design Thinking Frameworks

Through design thinking activities, students can strategically work to get to purpose through a process of active thinking and creative problem-solving. Though design thinking frameworks are relatively new to many educators, they have been applied to education for a long time. Don Buckley (Twitter and Instagram: @donbuckley) has been working in design thinking spaces since their inception, creating tools for educators to use (**Figure 1.5**). I asked him for his thoughts on design thinking in terms of social good in education. "Social good problems are complex and ambiguous," he shared. "Design thinking can be easy to teach, but it is as much about mindset as it is methods. Changing a mindset is changing behavior, and that's hard."

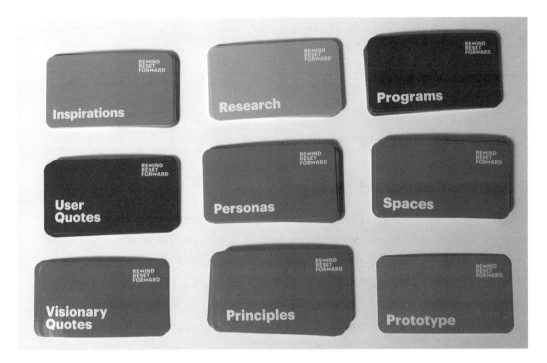

1.5 At rewind.reset. forward, Don Buckley develops tools for design thinking work.

Here are a few tenets of design thinking to consider as you develop your lessons and identify the skills you want to cultivate:

- embrace ambiguity

- build creative confidence

- create with empathy and optimism (IDEO, 2015)

Human-Centered Design

Human-centered design (HCD) is a form of design thinking. A three-phase approach to problem-solving and learning, it keeps the human central to all decision-making. Described and coined by Cooley (1980) and popularized by the Stanford d.school and the design firm IDEO (ideo.org), HCD builds upon participatory action research by offering proposed solutions to problems. Rooted in empathy and sincerity of thought, HCD moves students through these three phases:

1. **INSPIRATION.** In this phase, the students are immersed in context. They ask many questions and engage in observation, interviews, and journaling. This phase helps students understand how to get started before executing ideas. Here, learning is messy, exploratory, and centered on the people students ultimately want to help.

2. **IDEATION.** In the ideation phase, you and your students bring together and formulate ideas from the inspiration phase. Here you brainstorm many solutions to the established "problem" or steps toward meeting a goal.

3. **IMPLEMENTATION.** In the final phase of HCD, students prepare to execute concepts or ideas.

Human-centered design is meant to be a continuous process that encourages students to iterate and develop ideas over time. Students can create roadmaps, prototypes, peer-review feedback loops, and even pilots of their concepts.

In the classroom, you can use these three phases of HCD to guide students toward purpose in their efforts to improve the lives of others.

Here are a few human-centered design activities that can help your students establish purpose and get to the point of their project, prototype, or campaign.

INSPIRATION ACTIVITIES

As you prepare to begin work in social good, the inspiration phase is a good place to start. The Five Whys and the Card Sort are two exercises to get ideas flowing.

The Five Whys

The Five Whys is a way to help expand ideas and move beyond initial responses. The Five Whys technique was developed by the Toyota Motor Company in the 1950s as part of its problem-solving training (Ohno, 1988). For this activity, start by asking a student a question related to the work. Take the response and change it into a why question. Do this four times. The resulting responses should provide a deeper understanding and connection to the root cause or purpose. Here is a simplified example:

QUESTION 1: *In the story of the Three Little Pigs, why did the third pig build a house of bricks?*

RESPONSE 1: Because she wanted to have a strong house.

QUESTION 2: *Why did the third pig want to have a strong house?*

RESPONSE 2: Because she knew the wolf would try to blow it down.

QUESTION 3: *Why did she think the wolf would try to blow it down?*

RESPONSE 3: Because the wolf blew down the house of straw and the house of sticks.

QUESTION 4: *Why did the wolf blow down the house of straw and the house of sticks?*

RESPONSE 4: Because he wanted to get to the three pigs.

QUESTION 5: *Why did the wolf want to get to the three pigs?*

RESPONSE 5: Because he wanted to eat the pigs.

Even without background knowledge of the story, you can understand the third pig's intention, purpose, and motivation for building a strong house—she wanted to survive! As you and your students engage in The Five Whys activity, be sure questions and responses are recorded for future analysis.

Card Sorts

Card Sorts are one of my favorite activities for understanding student thinking routines and preferences. Card Sorts can be used with students of all ages and with any lesson, and offer a tangible, hands-on conversation starter. To conduct a Card Sort, add images, photos, sketches, or words to individual cards and follow these guidelines:

- one concept per card

- three to five cards total

- can be handwritten index cards or printed from a digital design

A simplified example might be preference of activity: art, music, makerspace, or research.

Art	Music	Makerspace	Research

1.6 This is an example of a card sort.

Hand the cards to a student and ask him or her to put them in order. Here, students may look at you for direction ("Order, as in . . .?"), but just say, "Please put them in an order that makes sense to you." After the student has ordered the cards, invite him or her to share the thinking behind the order. Why did the student prioritize one over the other? Why did he or she sort in that physical manner (horizontal, vertical, diagonal, in a stack, etc.)? As in The Five Whys, be sure to document responses.

IDEATION ACTIVITIES

Affinity mapping and journey mapping are two ideation activities to try out with your students.

Affinity Mapping

Affinity mapping is a great activity for classroom groups to do together. Use sticky notes or tech tools such as **Stickies.io** (stickies.io) or **Padlet** (padlet.com) for capturing and sharing ideas.

For the first part of the process, invite students to note as many answers to a question as possible (e.g., "How might our classroom contribute to the Earth Day celebration at our school next month?"). Let them know that ideas do not need to be completely formed—unfinished, incomplete, or even impossible is okay. The main point to get across for the first step is that there should only be one idea per sticky note.

After all ideas are added, either to an accessible wall space or virtual idea board, invite students to group ideas by association/likeness/affinity. If you have a large group, invite several representatives to lead the mapping by talking out loud and moving the stickies as they go.

At the conclusion of the activity, you should have several affinity groups and perhaps a few outliers. This helps to narrow ideas and options and provides synthesized understandings for the group. Final ideas could even be used in a Card Sort activity in the future.

Journey Mapping

To build a journey map, students will take an idea from the inspiration phase and map out a "user journey" (the steps a person would go through when interacting with the solution or experience). At the top of the paper, students should include a title and a brief description of the "end user profile" (i.e., a description of the person for whom they are designing or building). Words, short phrases, and images should capture ideas for the journey. Encourage students to use boxes and arrows as they go. The journey map can lead students to build an advocacy campaign, an invention, or even a sustainability program. Completed journey maps can be added to the design plans as artifacts of the process.

IMPLEMENTATION ACTIVITIES

Here are two activities to get you and your students into a start-up thought process: define success and prepare a pitch.

Define Success

In human-centered design, as with strong instructional design, success is clearly defined and detailed. This is of critical importance in innovation and invention, as ideas are often new and without exemplars or examples from experience. To help students define success for their design, have them consider and answer these questions:

1. What is the anticipated timeline of your project?

2. What are the steps in your roadmap?

3. What are the key objectives at each point?

4. What is your anticipated impact?

5. How do you plan to measure impact?

Answers to questions can be prepared in a presentation, illustration, or writing assignment.

Prepare Your Pitch

In business, developers create pitch presentations to share their ideas and their purpose in creating a new product, service, or program. As students finalize their ideas, roadmaps, and measures of success, guide them to create an elevator speech as an innovative method of sharing. Elevator speeches (sometimes called elevator pitches) are brief and focused statements created to spark interest in an idea. They are typically twenty to thirty seconds long (or about the length of a short elevator ride). The speech should clearly state the goal, vision, and anticipated impact, and end with an interesting question to encourage engagement. As students create their elevator speeches, have them work with classmates to practice and receive feedback. Give students an authentic audience by inviting a panel of parents or community members to hear the pitches and share advice, questions, and recognition. Record pitches with video and save for the future.

AFFIRMATION OF PURPOSE-DRIVEN PROJECTS

As mentioned previously, we as teachers have a responsibility to guide students in the process of learning. Our role, particularly in the process of design-thinking routines, is one of facilitation. My friend Koen Timmers (@zelfstudie), an educator in Belgium, says the teacher should be a "help desk" in the classroom, with the students discovering and constructing learning on their own.

Students who go through an exploratory process to discover purpose and then design projects or programs intentionally based on that purpose will look to you for a response. Your supportive comment will be an important one. Here are a few quick responses to encourage a growth mindset and build confidence and self-affirming beliefs:

- "Yes, and . . ." as opposed to "No."

- "How might we . . ." as opposed to "That won't work."

- "Have you researched . . ." as opposed to "That is incorrect."

Design Thinking at Scale: International School of Brussels

The International School of Brussels (ISB), located on a forty-acre campus near the city center of Brussels, Belgium, serves more than 1,500 students aged two to nineteen from sixty-two countries. As the educators at ISB work each day to meet the school mission of "everyone included, everyone challenged, everyone successful," they incorporate design thinking and student voice throughout all levels of learning. Here, David Willows (@davidwillows), Mike Crowley (@crowley_mike), and Mary Jeanne Farris (@mjfarris) of ISB share what they have learned.

At its most basic level—particularly in the field of education—innovation can be as simple as demonstrating a willingness to consider doing things differently, an openness to new thinking and potentially disruptive ideas, and a disposition to listen to beliefs and perspectives that may challenge our own. Our mission and beliefs about learning and innovation at ISB are framed by a set of research-based Learning Principles (**Figure 1.7**). The questions we are committed to continuously asking as a school are based on seeking the best possible contexts and opportunities for our learners as outlined in these principles.

Our Learning Principles and our Character Standards (Openness, Reflection, Resilience, Integrity, Fairness, Compassion) drove our initial research into design thinking. Developing engaged, connected, and empowered learners who were resilient, reflective, and open would require a shift in teaching, learning, and assessment. The design process aligned with these aspirations.

Incorporating inquiry cycles into learning requires educators to rethink how students develop and demonstrate understanding. Across several subject areas, teachers define the big understandings and use ISB's *Inquiry Cycle* to help students explore those ideas. We have clearly defined each stage of the process, and teachers monitor and assess student progress throughout. This shift has required professional development for teachers, paring down curriculum "to be covered," and a focus on what students really need to understand.

1.7

The International School of Brussels (ISB) has developed a set of learning principles that frame their mission and beliefs.

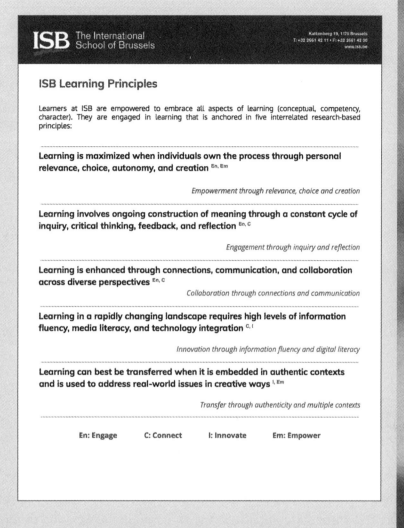

Most importantly, there are elements within the day-to-day experience at ISB that reflect its commitment to social good. Numerous service-learning activities, ample volunteering opportunities within the community, and an ethos of continuous improvement in all that the school sets out to do are testimonials of the school's public and transparent goal of creating a better world.

continued

continued

For schools thinking about adding design thinking, we would suggest starting with some of the following questions:

- What kinds of learners do we want to our students to be?

- What would learning in our school need to look like to meet that goal?

- What would we need to be explicitly teaching students to be successful?

- How will we support teachers and students to make this shift?

ISB's Major Learnings:

- We must continually challenge all of our assumptions about learning and school.

- Students are capable of great things if schools are willing to empower them.

- Change is an ongoing process that requires bold, committed leadership and constant dialogue.

To learn more about the work of the educators at ISB, check out the hashtag #ISBLbD.

DIGITAL CITIZENSHIP IN ACTION

After their work in the phases of inspiration, ideation, and implementation, your students will be armed with a purpose and prepared to move into planning for their next steps of action. Work in social good provides an opportunity for the immediate application of skills, so pedagogy and practice must move from preparing students for the future to plugging them into the world in front of them here and now. Instead of reading about the world, students can learn *with* the world, not just thinking in the abstract about digital citizenship and collaboration skills, but actually developing them. This moves us as educators to a place of designing experiences instead of scenarios.

Social good and social action require multi-level thinking. Students need to consider a variety of viewpoints, attitudes, and beliefs. They need to move from egocentric vantage points to seeing the world through the eyes of another—shifting from individual to community to global positions. To take action, they are required to be thoughtful, measured, inventive, and persistent—to have "stick-to-it-iveness," an essential skill of success, as my grandpa used to tell me.

Students today, already leveraging technology for communication, creative problem-solving, and organization of ideas, are independently beginning to use innovative technologies to work with the world in their personal lives. As digital citizens, students in our classrooms are proactive in sharing messages and perspectives. Through use of edtech for social good, we can meet them as co-learners to execute on solutions—their solutions—for a better world.

Power of Mobile Learning and Social Networking

Learning today is on the go! It is social and mobile, no longer isolated within classroom walls. Instead of a unidirectional teacher-to-student transmission of knowledge, learning now can be connected and participatory, allowing for discovery of themes and points of convergence. Networked mobile devices allow for anytime-anywhere learning and sharing, which empowers students to research, record, and relate:

- **RESEARCH.** Conduct online searches, access experts, find up-to-date information

- **RECORD.** Capture learning with photos, audio, and video, contribute to message boards and social media, curate information, ideas, and experiences

- **RELATE.** Assess the accuracy and credibility of sources, connect to other points of view, find relevance and relationship

Global Collaboration

Global collaboration provides the opportunity for students to connect with people around the world from different backgrounds, cultures, and traditions. By communicating and collaborating across lines of difference, student learning can be informed and enriched, broadened and expanded.

Formats and Practices for Engagement

To minimize barriers that may arise when collaborating with international groups, work with your students to consider practices for effective engagement:

- Awareness of and respect for cultural practices and norms.

- Consideration of access and reliability of WiFi connection. (Be sure to have back-up plans ready!)

- Meeting options: Synchronous (meeting together at the same time either in person or online) vs. asynchronous (communicating digitally with each other with time delays in formats such as email, video-recorded messages, or text messages).

Digital Tools

As students move beyond introductions and into true collaboration, there are many tools that can facilitate their global communications and help them bring their social action projects or inquiries to the world.

- **COMMUNICATION: WhatsApp** (whatsapp.com), **Voxer** (voxer.com), **Remind** (remind.com)

- **VIDEOCONFERENCING: Skype** (skype.com), **Zoom** (zoom.us/education), **Google Hangouts** (hangouts.google.com)

- **TRANSLATION: Google Translate** (translate.google.com), **Bing Translator** (bing.com/translator)

- **SCHEDULING:** Email for coordination of times, **Doodle** (doodle.com)

- **WORKFLOW:** **Trello** (trello.com), **Padlet** (padlet.com)

- **DATA COLLECTION AND ANALYSIS:** **Google Sheets** (google.com/sheets), **Microsoft Excel** (products.office.com/en-us/excel)

- **DOCUMENTATION:** **Google Docs** (google.com/docs), **Microsoft Word** (microsoft.com)

- **CURATION:** **Wakelet** (wakelet.com), **Evernote** (evernote.com), **Feedly** (feedly.com), **Pocket** (getpocket.com)

- **GAMES FOR GOOD:** **Freerice** (freerice.com), **Spent** (playspent.org)

- **MULTI-PLAYER GAMES:** **Minecraft** (minecraft.net), **Kahoot!** (kahoot.com)

Virtual Reality Field Trips

Though not a replacement for real-life experience through travel and cultural immersion, virtual reality (VR) can be used to augment learning and expand understanding. Virtual environments offer 3D views into new worlds. Accessible through mobile devices, web links, or virtual reality headsets, VR can cross all content areas in education, including humanities and social studies, geography, literacy and language, science, arts, physical education, and math.

To enhance and inform the social good and social action work of your students, organize virtual reality field trips.

STEP 1: Select destination.

Have students determine a place or population of people they want to "visit" for their VR field trip.

- **By geographic location.** Better understand homelessness in El Salvador, overpopulation in the megacity of Mumbai, effects of pollution on underwater coral reefs

- **By perspective.** See the world through the eyes of an architect or sculptor, as a father in a refugee camp, as an eighty-year-old cancer patient

STEP 2: Determine objectives.

Help establish purpose and meaning by preparing a list of objectives. What do you anticipate you will see? What will you be searching for? How will the VR field trip give you a deeper understanding of the human experience? How will this new learning impact your current project/work? Without specific goals and outcomes in mind for the VR field trip, the experience could become a simple tech activity.

STEP 3: "Head out" for your VR field trip.

- For younger students, you can build excitement, "pack your bags," and head in. Website VR experiences projected on walls or screens are great for groups.

- For older students, encourage them to work independently and explore environments on a personal level. Mobile devices, headsets, and smartphones work well for this.

Some of my favorite VR programs include **Nearpod VR** (nearpod.com/nearpod-vr) and **Google Expeditions** (edu.google.com/products/vr-ar/expeditions).

STEP 4: Reflect.

Following the VR field trip, engage students in a reflection circle to debrief on the experience and share new or enhanced understandings of the world. What was surprising? What questions remain? How will your new views into the world impact the roadmap of your current projects?

TAKE ACTION
PLAN TO JOIN A GLOBAL PROJECT

Ready to dive into planning for global collaboration with your students? Here are a few of my favorite global projects and global activities:

- **Empatico Virtual Exchange** (empatico.org). Virtual exchange platform for K-6 grade classrooms with lessons focused on sparking empathy (see Appendix C for more information)

- **The Goals Project** (goalsproject.org). Annual September global project inviting PK—college educators to join teams with sixteen other classrooms; each class covers one of the SDGs (Global Goals) and shares with the whole team by email

- **Mystery Skype** (education.microsoft.com/skype-in-the-classroom /mystery-skype). Use of videoconferencing to guess the location of partner classrooms by asking yes/no questions and using maps and other resources; appropriate for students of all ages

- **Global Oneness Project** (globalonenessproject.org). Videos and lesson plans for high school and college students focused on cultural and environmental issues

- **Teens Dream Co Lab** (teensdreamcolab.org). Community of teens who meet in videoconference rooms to discuss global issues and sustainability

- **The Global Read Aloud** (theglobalreadaloud.com). Six-week global collaboration project held each fall; classrooms read and share on a yearly book selection

- **Rock Your World** (rock-your-world.org). Human rights advocacy campaign program for middle school and high school students (see Appendix C for more information)

- **World's Largest Lesson** (worldslargestlesson.globalgoals.org). Yearly lesson plan for the world around one of the Global Goals (see Appendix C for more information)

BOLD INVITATION
DESIGN A GLOBAL PROJECT

Designing a global project may sound like quite a commitment, but it is easier than you might think. To start a global project, all you need are (1) a lesson you have created (and in most cases have taught before and loved) and (2) the desire to bring students from outside your classroom into the lesson. You can use free tech tools and a global network of teachers to get your project up and running. Here is one way to get a global project started and out to the world:

STEP 1: Select a project you have created that you hope to do with your students.

STEP 2: Use tools such as **Adobe Spark** (spark.adobe.com) or **Weebly** (weebly.com) to create a free website. On your new site, share photos, ideas for the project, and a timeline with important project dates.

STEP 3: Invite others to join you. You can email colleagues in different parts of the world (or even from neighboring schools or classrooms next door). Create a hashtag to represent the project and share it with the link to your site on Twitter and Facebook.

STEP 4: Kick off your global project with the participating classrooms. Be sure to document the journey on your website. Consider **QuadBlogging** (quadblogging.net), in which students from four different classrooms co-author a blog.

STEP 5: End with a celebration! Use the project as a starting point for a continued classroom-to-classroom friendship.

MY PEACEMAKER PROFILE ACTIVITY #1
A STORYBOARD

Storyboarding is a prototyping method that stems from video production. As a filmmaker sets out to shoot a video, she or he may storyboard ideas to visually represent frames or shots or scenes. In education, teachers can use storyboards with students to serve as visual maps of anticipated plans for a project or design. Most often used in the ideation phase of human-centered design, storyboarding allows ideas to unfold in sequence, helping to identify anticipated roadblocks or missing steps.

To begin, think through the process of how you will guide your students to take action for social good. Will you encourage them to create a campaign? Do you hope to join a global project? Is there a schoolwide program you have all been wanting to develop? Use the template shown here in **Figure 1.8** (you can also download it from jenwilliamsedu.com/peacemaker-profile.html), create your own with hand-drawn squares to represent stages, or create a digital storyboard using design edtech tools such as **Canva** (canva.com) or **Storyboarder** (wonderunit.com/storyboarder). Include a project title and then use each square (frame) as a step in the process you are planning. The template here includes six frames, but feel free to use more if needed. Save your storyboard in a binder or digitally in a file, as this will be the first part of your profile that you will develop through the rest of this book.

My PeaceMAKER Profile

Activity #1

Using Edtech for Social Good Storyboard

Project:

1.8 My PeaceMAKER Profile Activity #1

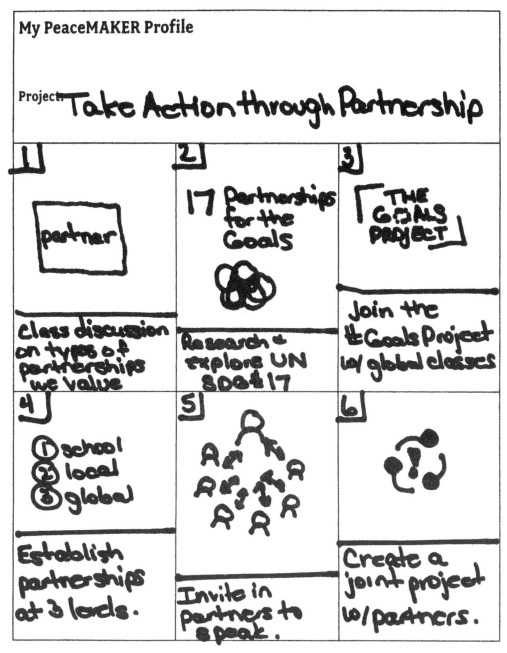

My PeaceMAKER Profile

Project: **Take Action through Partnership**

1 partner

Class discussion on types of partnerships we value

2 17 Partnerships for the Goals

Research & explore UN SDG # 17

3 THE GOALS PROJECT

Join the #Goals Project w/ global classes

4 ① school ② local ③ global

Establish partnerships at 3 levels.

5

Invite in partners to speak.

6

Create a joint project w/ partners.

1.9 My PeaceMAKER Profile Activity #1 Example . (Templates and examples for all My PeaceMAKER Profile activities can be found at jenwilliamsedu.com/peacemaker-profile.html.)

2

THE TIME YOU GIVE TO THE THINGS YOU VALUE

The greatest challenge in committing to social good and innovation may be finding room for them in our lives and schedules. This chapter focuses on the educator's use of time and how to determine and prioritize the activities you value most so that you can enter more fully into social change and global collaboration.

Generational Peace by Kaitlyn Zong, Grade 11
Medium: Pencil
Educators: Aaron Yetter, Heather Morningstar, Randy Ziegenfuss
Salisbury High School, Allentown, PA, USA

INSPIRATION: Sometimes, You've Just Got to Jump in!

"Your efforts to work collaboratively as educators are a good start. Though if we are going to reach these global goals, we must find ways to move beyond collaboration and instead join together in solidarity." These powerful words have stayed with me ever since I heard them spoken by Grenada's then-ambassador to the United Nations, Dessima Williams—her hands together, fingers interlaced and firmly locked. This word "solidarity" continues to echo in my mind since the meeting that day.

I remember standing outside the United Nations building with my colleagues after our meeting with Ambassador Williams. We stood on the steps, the flags of the world moving in unison in the cold New York City January wind. Tasked by Ambassador Williams and a team of UN delegates to find ways to use education to help realize the Sustainable Development Goals, my colleagues and I knew we needed to do something, anything; we were just not sure what. I said, "How about we start with a hashtag?" And, at that moment, #TeachSDGs began.

Charged with advancing the work of the UN in relation to education through advocacy and outreach, we soon recognized that our group of four educators, all from North America, was far from representative of a world that knew many definitions of teacher, school, and system. To meet a universal call to action that ensures no one would be left behind, we needed more voices. With no more than a hashtag and a little determination, we set out to find other teachers who were ready to mobilize and join us in our grassroots efforts to help reach the seventeen global goals that hold a promise of transforming our world.

UN Sustainable Development Goal 4 (SDG4): Quality Education focuses specifically on education and seeks to ensure inclusive and equitable quality education and promote lifelong learning opportunities for all. However, educators today must engage with all the goals, because our classrooms have students who know poverty and hunger, inequality and injustice. As teachers, we take action for the climate and for clean water, and we seek well-being and peace for our students and for all citizens of our world. We, by the design of our profession, must be focused on all the goals.

The complexity of the global goals demands sound infrastructure and unified vision. Inspired by Sustainable Development Goal 17 (SDG17): Partnership for the Goals, we as the cofounders of #TeachSDGs developed a plan to prioritize time, process, and coherence in our efforts to bring global educators together in conversation and cooperation to transform the world. We believed it was critical to be aware of our privilege and perspective, and we worked to move beyond our networks and empower the voices of others.

Four soon grew to seventeen, which then, through a process of pledge-taking and social following, expanded to more than 30,000 global educators. Lines on a map that connected #TeachSDGs now cross oceans, continents, and borders and pass through beautiful lands with names such as Tunisia, Saudi Arabia, Costa Rica, Romania, Ghana, Iran, and Sri Lanka and into cities named Abu Dhabi, Bangkok, Paris, Akungba Akoko, San Diego, Islamabad, Buenos Aires, and Brussels.

Just as the global goals belong to each and every citizen of the world, we believe that #TeachSDGs belongs to all educators.

Each day, educators go to TeachSDGs.org and take the pledge to teach the Sustainable Development Goals, and we are working to provide the resources our ambassadors and others need to get the message out to those who may not have access to technology or reliable information.

Bit by bit, we move forward through partnership and in solidarity. We dedicate time in our days and commit to keeping with the words shared with us by Ambassador Williams: "Let us not waste the opportunity."

POINT OF CONTACT: TIME, EDUCATION, AND INNOVATION

The concept of time may be one of the most misunderstood elements of innovation—and in this increasingly advanced digital age, the greatest challenge in innovation may be finding how to fit it into our lives and schedules.

Time has always been a critical component of educational models. Prior to 1850, the learning in one-room schoolhouses offered lessons rooted in patience and intentionality. Commitment of time was distributed based on necessity with connections to responsibility, diligence, and survival. The pace was predictable; schedules reflected a desire for order and repetition. Time then was slow and steady.

Near the end of the nineteenth century, the Industrial Revolution pulled education into the age of efficiency and operations. Management principles of factory models were applied as mass public schooling programs came into existence. Children began shifting rooms and/or topics every fifty minutes at the ring of a bell, and soon time, productivity, and progress blurred into coexistence. And there, for quite some time, much of the world of education remained.

Enter the digital age. Life sped up. Quickly.

In response, our world has had to catch up and keep up. Work and life, intersecting and innovating, are in constant motion. Work has shifted to prioritize flexibility, creativity, and process as opposed to the number of outputs from production. With a need for questioning, ideation, and commerce of thought, we are back to figuring out the hows and whats and whys of time in relation to the work of today.

In modern education, I've found that discussions around time show up in three main places: (1) in schedule planning (most often an activity that happens once per year or once every few years with small groups of select individuals); (2) in lesson plans, as the number of minutes a teacher anticipates students in a class will need to complete a learning activity; and (3) in sentences that are less about the use of time and more about the lack of it (e.g., "There isn't enough time," "We are out of time," "If I only had more time.").

We are in an interesting and pivotal moment in education. As the technological landscape of our world changes and evolves, educators and students are beginning to examine current systems, processes, and routines of schooling. Together, they are creating new ways—better ways—that match their needs. They are seeking out and finding necessary resources and support, and they are boldly changing our world.

And time—specifically our use of time—has secured its spot as an essential element of innovative and transformational teaching and learning.

WHERE TO JUMP IN, WHERE TO SLOW DOWN, WHERE TO SPEED UP

Innovation does not begin at point zero. It is dynamic, sometimes quiet and sometimes noisy, oftentimes messy. Innovation can challenge assumptions, or it can confirm that current ways are nearly optimal and just in need of a little tweaking. Though innovation can be a departure from past practices or beliefs, it is not dismissive of the decisions and mindsets and paths that have been taken to get to now. Innovation is an evolution of thoughts and actions, informed by history and experience and fueled by questions and problems.

Innovation is not reserved only for those aiming for large-scale disruption. It includes people who take action on new ideas in their own small, incremental ways. From little moments of inquiry to taking action to bring about collective change for humanity—with innovation and social good, there is a place for everyone.

But for many educators, the question of how to begin can be overwhelming.

I remember being a little girl and thinking about the universe and its vastness. It was dizzying to imagine where it started and where it extended to. What was beyond, and where did we fit in? I would have to push myself out of those thoughts to get myself centered again.

Over my years as an educator, I've had a similar feeling when thinking about education and change and where my work fits in. How might I make an impact? Where will I leave my mark? Can I make things better? The simple answer that always brings me solace and keeps me going is my students; probably many other teachers feel the same. But even with that inspiration, our work can feel arduous when so much focus is on debates—such as sweeping reform and a need for fixing so-called broken systems—that are immense and often seemingly beyond our reach as individual educators.

But one day, my thoughts were channeled when I read a single sentence that Sal Khan, author and founder of Khan Academy, had tucked into the chapter "Questioning Customs" in his 2013 book *The One World School House: Education Reimagined*:

> Like every other system put in place by human beings, education is an invention, a work in progress. (Khan, 2013)

That one sentence made all the difference for me.

Education as an invention. From its outset, education was something created with thought and intention, out of a desire to make life better. It was a development based on the best available resources and models of progress and advancement known at that moment, but as with any invention, its use over time has revealed new ways for it to provide value. It made sense to me to see education not as broken or damaged or impervious to re-engineering, but instead as something in progress, ready to be reimagined and retooled. Considering education as an invention allowed me to escape from paralyzed thought and propelled me into motion, ready to take part in improving something that was once a unique idea—an innovation of its time.

So, returning to the question of how to begin, let's consider these three areas:

Where to Jump In

Decisions about where to jump in and what to focus on will be extremely personal and will vary from classroom to classroom (and possibly from year to year). The constants should be you and your students. The work you do and the time you dedicate to that work can be guided by interests, by passions, or in some cases by a response to a distress signal or unanticipated call for help. Sometimes, knowing precisely where to jump in may be evident, but more often it is not. Bold change can start big, and bold change can start small. You just need to be ready to start.

Where to Slow Down

I began this chapter by stating that I think that the concept of time in innovation is often misunderstood. For us to innovate in education and bring about positive change in our world, it is going to take time, and it is going to take action. At a basic level, I view innovation as movement in a forward, positive direction. The rate of speed, though, can vary.

Innovation doesn't necessarily require that we move quickly. In fact, research shows that rushed and hurried learning can lead to superficial levels of understanding. Determining your areas of focus through a thoughtful process of collaborative inquiry and with co-construction of driving questions can enable you to understand where to spend more time and what to emphasize in instruction. You may find you need to drop some things (lessons, items on your schedule, etc.) to make room for depth in learning and doing. In fact, the skills of prioritizing and focus can *become the learning* through the process of innovation.

Where to Speed Up

I've found that opportunities to speed up present themselves naturally in innovation—often in bright, flashing neon colors, joyously proclaiming "Hold on. Here we go!" The tricky part is being ready to clear a path for those bursts of charged and productive action when they arrive. Here is where statements such as "time is up" or "we need to move on" can quash creativity and lead to fragmented learning and progress. Just as we as educators need to be conscious of what needs to stay and what can go when we're thinking about where to slow down, it will be important for us to be critically selective and responsive in times of acceleration.

As we ask ourselves where we can jump in and where we should speed up, it may be as simple as recognizing our roles as educators who are:

- fiercely protective of times of increased student engagement,

- consciously mindful of the presence of flow, and

- boldly aware of the need for flexibility in time and in thought.

INNOVATIONS IN THE USE OF TIME

In recent years, classrooms, schools, and districts have begun experimenting with innovations in the use of time. Moving beyond single lessons and projects, they are making long-term commitments to schedule changes and allocation of resources, technologies, and new methods of teaching, often to facilitate action on social good and transformative learning. Here are a few:

Genius Hour

Inspired by Google's practice of 20% Time (encouraging employees to commit 20% of their work week to exploring new ideas of their choice based on interest), Genius Hour is an instructional practice that provides dedicated time each week (or each day) for classrooms to prioritize curiosity and creativity through individualized passion projects. Genius Hour harnesses inquiry-based, student-driven learning and offers a structured format that invites students to dream without limits and take action on big ideas. Teachers act as guides to get students asking questions that matter to them and then to help them get organized to learn by doing.

There are several frameworks and step-by-step plans to support teachers and schools in implementing this type of practice. In the book *Genius Hour: Passion Projects that Ignite Innovation and Student Inquiry* (2017), educator Andi McNair shares six Ps of Genius Hour, which can help students create and carry out their projects:

1. Passion

2. Pitch

3. Plan

4. Project

5. Product

6. Presentation

To learn more about Genius Hour, be sure to check in with educators sharing ideas on Twitter with the hashtag #GeniusHour. You can follow Andi, too, on Twitter at @mcnairan3.

Virtual Exchange

Virtual exchange involves using technology to connect groups in different locations to communicate, collaborate, and exchange information. In education, virtual exchange provides opportunities to move beyond the walls of the classroom by using collaborative technologies and innovative teaching practices to promote global citizenship, build digital literacy skills, and cultivate appreciation of diverse viewpoints. Virtual exchange can be a part of the instruction of any content area and requires only a single device and reliable internet connection.

Through creative use of time in synchronous (real-time) and asynchronous (delayed response) interactions, classrooms can connect with individuals who may represent different cultures, experiences, or belief systems. Incorporating virtual exchange into instruction allows for authentic and meaningful practice, building essential skills such as empathy and kindness as well as critical thinking and cooperation.

Ada McKim (@Ada_McKim), a high school teacher in Canada, recalls her first experience using Skype with her 2011 World Issues class:

> We sang and danced and learned from orphaned peers in Uganda. Weeks later, after funding a community garden and seeing its early growth, we listened to our new friends lament a lack of rain that was likely to destroy the crops. Such drought was becoming increasingly common. We were learning about climate change at the time, and this tragic real-life example sank into all of our souls.

Within digital environments, we can learn about the world with the world and we can begin to remove dangerous barriers of access, bias, prejudice, and indifference by developing relationships and finding connections. Virtual exchange moves us beyond just showing up. Instead, time spent together in virtual exchange allows students to take action—locally, globally, and boldly.

Moonshots

Energized to take a risk: ✓

Fearless and determined: ✓

A little bit radical: ✓

Bursting to try something different and audacious: ✓

Then, moonshots are for you!

The concept of a "moonshot" originated in 1962 when President John F. Kennedy told an audience at Rice University about his dream to land a man on the moon within eight years. Was it possible? He didn't know. But by bringing together the right people with the right skills, the right mindsets, and the right tools at the right time, the U.S. space program soon showed the world how a vision built on hope and paired with strategy could bring about incredible results. And, with the 1969 manned moon landing, moonshots would forever change how the world approached ingenuity and innovative thought.

Today, some bold and courageous educators are adapting moonshot approaches to problem-solving, creativity, and computational thinking and bringing them to classroom spaces. And they are looking at innovations in today's industry to help guide the way.

At X Development, Google's moonshot factory, innovators and makers of the future find and take on the world's largest problems using a three-phase process:

1. Address a big problem.

2. Propose a radical solution.

3. Integrate needed technologies.

By putting charged energy into deliberate planning and messy experimentation, they seek solutions that may impact the lives of billions of people. Tasked with considering and narrowing down more than one hundred worthy projects per year, their team offers their key to successful moonshots: "Moonshots don't begin with brainstorming clever answers. They start with the hard work of finding the right questions" (Thompson, 2017).

Eager to get going on moonshots? Test out some moonshot-inspired practices ready for teaching and learning:

- **EMBRACE BOUNDLESS LEARNING.** Take on ambitious projects void of expectation or certainty of outcome. Practice curiosity over judgment.

- **GET SERIOUS ABOUT STUDENT-GENERATED QUESTIONS.** Dedicate lessons to the skill and art of questioning. Model effective use of questions and share your own process of composing them. After interacting with content or media, collaborate on questions as a class. Shift from seeking answers to generating questions together.

- **FIND VALUE IN THE LEARNING THAT OCCURS THROUGH MOONSHOT PROPOS-ALS.** Dedicate time to activities that develop effective communication of ideas, active listening, and providing, receiving, and applying feedback.

- **CONTEMPLATE HOW YOUR WORK CAN POSITIVELY IMPACT PEOPLE.** Who are the people? What are their stories? How can invention transform their days and their lives?

- **TALK WITH STUDENTS ABOUT WHAT LEARNING COULD LOOK LIKE IF YOU WENT THROUGH X'S THREE-PHASE PROCESS.** What might that look like in your learning space?

Be sure to check out X and their inventions for the global good of all at **x.company**.

Reflective Classroom Cultures

At the heart of innovation and social good are purpose, empathy, and a strong desire to make a positive difference in the lives of people. Because we often focus on the work and its potential impact, we dedicate a large amount of time to the project itself—but not always to reflection on the process. Due to time constraints, curricular and scheduling demands, or even the excitement of completing a project and being done, it is easy to neglect one of the most important parts of inquiry and innovation: the debrief.

The debrief. The reflection. The how-did-it-go conversation. Without this type of pause, we miss opportunities to identify what went well and to grow by dissecting areas of challenge. In many instances, reflection brings the most powerful learning.

Reflection breathes life into past experiences and unleashes new, unanticipated ideas. Moments when we say, "Wait, I didn't consider that," or, "Oh, hold on, we need to try again," can transform the end of one task into the beginning of another. And to build a reflective classroom culture, all you need to do is be bold in preserving and protecting time.

"We continue daily to assess what we offer students in our district as well as how it's offered," says Stephen Peters, superintendent of Laurens County School District 55 in South Carolina. "Opportunities to learn and grow are directly tied to the directions and decisions our students make about their present and future." As a leader, author, and speaker, Stephen works to share his message of attaining educational equity. He opens up pathways to show students that they matter (and are essential) in this world. For him, it is more than talk—it is about taking action, reflecting, and taking more action. In his district, he developed the widely recognized and awarded Ladies and Gentlemen's Clubs to help students develop self-confidence, self-belief, and a reflective culture. And in 2017, he starred with his students in the National Geographic documentary series, *American High School*. The issues in the episodes, as seen through the eyes of American students in their reflections, opened up conversations of race and class relations, education policy, friendship and heartache, and humanity.

Paying Attention to "Goosebump Moments"

In education, we are in the business of thinking: building knowledge, developing minds, supporting new learning. Even though we as educators are committed to developing productive, compassionate citizens of our world, our time in instruction seems to go primarily to content-area lessons. Now though, innovation and student-centered learning designs have given us freedom to expand our roles, so our instructional time reflects that we are really in the business of thinking and feeling.

What drives and motivates our students? How do they act on areas of interest? What are they most passionate about and why? What are their biggest hopes for their futures and for our world?

How do we as educators react to the feelings of our students? How might we design instruction to drive new forms of learning that can leave positive imprints on our students for their lifetimes? How can we demonstrate to our students that we are listening, and how can we let them know that they matter?

I've been asking myself these questions more and more. In the past several years, I have incorporated two practices into my instruction and into my life to try to catch up with the humanistic and social-emotional parts of my role.

First, in developing students' hearts and minds so that they're prepared to activate on change, I found that adjusting one question changes the entire lesson. Instead of asking "What do you think?" I lead with "How do you feel?" And then I pause and wait. The results are pretty spectacular. Be aware, though, that it may take time, modeling, and lots of practice to move students beyond responses of "good" or "fine." It can also be useful to let students answer the questions "How do you feel?" or "How does that make you feel?" by using different modes of expression (e.g., sketching, typed responses, video responses, or even back-channeled emojis on a message board).

Second, in addition to actively listening to my students, I have become more conscious of my own emotions—particularly my reactions to world events, social needs and human rights, and new ideas that are strong enough to evoke a positive physical response: butterflies in our stomachs, goosebumps on our arms.

"Goosebump moments," I call them—those times when someone tells you something so amazing, so special; the moments when you witness a beautiful act of humanity or kindness or joy; something that you notice and say, "That just gave me goosebumps." Typically, the adrenaline that caused the physical reaction quickly dissipates, and we just move on. But I believe there—right there—is where we need to remain, even if for only a few seconds. Pay attention, take note, come back to that feeling. Keep the *why* of that moment close and use it as a powerful inspiration for new ideas of innovation.

USING TIME TO ESTABLISH CLASS CULTURE AND NORMS

When we design a class schedule, we can build in activities that support a positive class culture. Here are three that use time to enhance interactions and build respect:

1. Value of a Name

2. Virtual Handshake

3. What's on Your Mind?

Value of a Name

2.1 Take the My Name, My Identity pledge to earn your digital badge.

A person's name is a declaration of self, with names tied to identity. Take time with students to explore the meanings and origins of student names through conversation and meaningful use of technology. Look to the organization **My Name, My Identity** (mynamemyidentity.org) for free lesson plans and projects that guide students to investigate the world, recognize different perspectives, communicate ideas, and take action. As an educator, you can visit the site and join with thousands of other educators by taking the online pledge to respect student names and pronounce them correctly.

Here are some ideas for the classroom recommended by My Name, My Identity (2016):

- Have students use multimedia to create presentations about their names or a family member's name, and request feedback on the presentation from someone who comes from a different cultural background.

- Have students create an infographic on the origin of a name.

- Have students make presentations on the naming convention in a culture other than their own.

Visit the **NameCoach** website (name-coach.com/namebadge) for free name pronunciation activities. Students can voice record their names online so others can easily learn and remember how to say them. A digital badge can be created and attached to any online profile or website.

Virtual Handshake

A handshake is a customary greeting between friends new and old. In digital spaces and when using advanced technologies, we must be thoughtful in finding ways to preserve relationship-building practices, such as greetings that can help build trust, camaraderie, and, ultimately, friendship.

2.2 Oluwaseun Kayode (4th grade teacher in Nigeria) and Wendy Turner (Delaware Teacher of the Year, elementary teacher) shared photos of their virtual exchanges.

A virtual handshake is a great way to begin any virtual exchange experience. Take time in the get-to-know-you activities, just as you would in person. After a synchronous virtual handshake meetup (check out Zoom, Google Hangouts, Whereby.com, or Skype as videoconferencing options), invite your students to follow up asynchronously by:

- Sending personalized messages with Adobe Spark videos

- Leaving voice recorded messages using Flipgrid, WhatsApp, or Voxer to elaborate on discussion topics

- Emailing photos or digitally accessorized photo creations (think photos with GIFs, text, icons, hyperlinks, etc.)

What's on Your Mind

Exit tickets as a reflective practice have become increasingly popular and useful for teachers looking to gauge learning through formative levels of assessment. I find that entry tickets can be just as valuable. One of my favorite entry/exit ticket activities is asking students to share visually through the use of technology how they are feeling or what is on their minds.

With collaborative technologies such as **Nearpod**'s Draw It feature (nearpod. com), teachers can upload PDFs of line drawings of heads and have students fill them up with images ("How do you feel?") or words ("What's on your mind?"). Depending on the group of students and the activity, I sometimes share images (without student names) with the class and ask for feedback and discussion.

This type of tech-supported mindfulness activity allows every student to contribute and express ideas. By watching responses per student over time, you can identify patterns of emotions that can serve as formative assessment data in building a full learning portfolio of a student.

2.3 These images were created in response to "How do you feel?" and "What's on your mind?" using Nearpod's Draw It feature.

TAKE ACTION
COMMIT TIME TO ACTION

Determine an area in which you want to commit time and take action, then share your commitment publicly. For example, you can tweet it out using the hashtag #TeachBoldly, you can print an image of your pledge and post it in your classroom, or you can research options on where you can take a public pledge. Here are a few pledges for taking action on social good:

- Pledge to **#TeachSDGs**: teachsdgs.org

- Pledge to **Act Now** on climate change: un.org/en/actnow

- Pledge to say student names correctly with **My Name, My Identity**: mynamemyidentity.org

- Find a global area of interest at **Global Citizen** and take the offered pledge: globalcitizen.org/en

BOLD INVITATION
WILL YOU WORK WITH ME? ACTIVITY

There is power in the question, "Will you work with me on this?" This question invites collaboration, innovation, inquiry, and change. Consider one of your big ideas or "moonshots" and invite someone in your school or community or in the world to join you.

Who will you invite? How will you include others in your conversation? Now is the time for teachers to join together to create contexts that empower all voices and to commit time to the work we value—the work that led us to become teachers, our calling to make a difference in the lives of children and in the world.

MY PEACEMAKER PROFILE ACTIVITY #2
ME IN A PIE CHART

Charts, tables, and graphs. Capturing data and visualizing concepts make for a happy teacher! So how might you document your commitment of time to the things you as an educator value most? If you were to write out your schedule for a typical school week, would it represent the things you value in education, in your district and school missions, and in your own professional instructional objectives?

A few years ago, I started doing the Me in a Pie Chart exercise with groups of educators. The concept is simple: you identify the areas to which you most want to commit time in your practice, research, study, and action, and then you create a visual representation of those areas. The objective is to align the way you spend your day with the things you value most.

I have found that the key to creating a Me in a Pie Chart is to be present. You could easily come up with a few things you are passionate about and drop them onto a graph, but transformative change will happen when you push past those initial ideas. When we go deeper, synthesize, and get at the essence of purpose, we can find greater meaning in how we value our time and our work.

Here is how it went for me when I did my own pie chart. I took time to determine my areas of focus, and I settled on three areas. Next, I thought about how I would like to distribute my time. I decided I wanted each area to carry equal weight (each of the three areas representing one third of my time). To finish up and share my commitment, I made this digital representation of my ideas.

Check out mine and then get ready for your second My PeaceMAKER Profile Activity—part of the foundational groundwork for the work ahead in activities three through six.

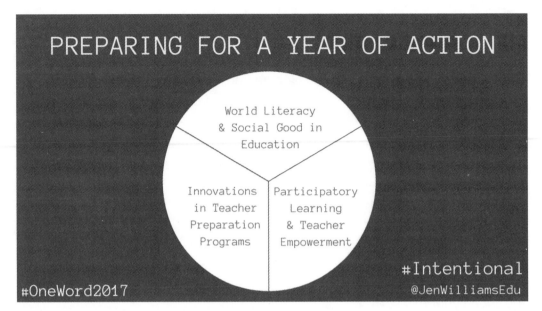

PREPARING FOR A YEAR OF ACTION

World Literacy & Social Good in Education

Innovations in Teacher Preparation Programs

Participatory Learning & Teacher Empowerment

#Intentional
@JenWilliamsEdu

#OneWord2017

2.4 This is how I allocated my time in my Me in a Pie Chart digital artifact.

STEP 1: Determine your timeframe

For me, it is convenient to think in terms of one year (one school year or one calendar year, depending on when you are creating your pie chart), but for you and your circumstances, it may make more sense to work in semesters or even multiple years. Let *manageable* and *sustainable* be your guides here, and don't have the length of time be too short or too long.

STEP 2: Identify the areas of progress that you value

Here is where "being present" will matter the most. In an ideal world, how would you as an educator hope to spend your time? What areas of professional practice do you value the most? Think big here. Keep your ideas centered on hopes and feelings, and resist letting your thoughts drift to your current schedule or to any barriers.

Just be sure to record your ideas: sticky notes between classes, voice recordings on your phone during recess, writing quick messages in your planner, and so on.

STEP 3: Synthesize and narrow

After you record your ideas, the next step is to get them organized. Pull together ideas that have natural affinity (remember affinity mapping from chapter 1) or relationships, set aside ones that may not work for now, and prioritize the ones that immediately make you feel, "This one for sure!" As themes emerge, give them new value titles if needed. Set your final ideas, stand back for a second, and ask yourself, "How do I feel?" I like to work with three big ideas, but you may land on fewer or more.

STEP 4: Move from ideation to implementaton

Okay! You have your big ideas! Now, it is time to determine how you want to allot your percentages of time. The only requirement is that they add up to 100%.

Let's say you have four ideas and you want to divide the time you dedicate to them equally (25% x 4 = 100%). Or, perhaps one big idea will take more of your focus so the distribution will be varied (e.g., 40% + 20% + 20% + 20% = 100%). Or (there is always someone who loves this method) you may find it fun and valuable to experiment with creative calculation (e.g., 38% + 32% + 16% + 14% = 100%—checked my math on that one!). It only needs to make sense to you and add up to 100%.

2.5 There are many ways to distribute time in a Me in a Pie Chart, as long as the slices add up to 100%.

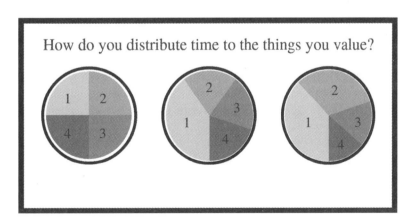

How do you distribute time to the things you value?

STEP 5: Use edtech to tell the story

With your big ideas and percentages set, you are ready to create your Me in a Pie Chart illustration. There are many different tools you can use to create your digital pie chart, but my favorites (all free) are:

- **Adobe Spark** (spark.adobe.com)

- **Canva** (canva.com)

- **Google Slides** (google.com/slides)

Be sure to add a title ("Me in a Pie Chart"), the time frame (maybe the year or semester), your identifying information (name and/or Twitter handle), and labels for each slice of your pie chart. Colors and fonts matter, so find ones that you love and that help tell the story of your big ideas that you value.

STEP 6: Share your story with an authentic audience

Who will be your authentic audience, the people with whom you can share your Me in a Pie Chart story? Some faculty may do this exercise as a team and share the results in person or on a school message board, whether digital (e.g., a Learning Management System like Canvas or Schoology) or analog (the good ole bulletin board). If you create your Me in a Pie Chart on your own, you can share it with your instructional team or school Professional Learning Community (PLC), with your students, or with your own Professional Learning Network (PLN). Consider sharing on Twitter, using the hashtag #PeaceMAKER and #TeachBoldly to bring your ideas to others who are sharing.

STEP 7: Connect your ideas to your practice

Take action on your ideas by applying them to your practice. How do the percentages on your Me in a Pie Chart correspond to your actual use of time? If you look at your weekly calendar with activities mapped and recorded, do you find that you are giving adequate time to the things you value? Are you able to identify areas where you could redirect time to work on your big ideas?

Start to highlight ways and times to take action. (I take "highlighting" to a literal level and color-code my big ideas, then color in blocks of time/areas of content.) Be sure to be patient and present in this part of the process.

STEP 8: Check in and reflect

Check in with yourself and with the group of people with whom you originally shared your pie chart (your "accountability partners"). Remember that even when we pursue innovation and take action on social good, life happens. Be kind to yourself and keep at it.

EXTENSION: Me in a Pie Chart with students

After you have tested out the process of narrowing your own big ideas, you can take the activity to the classroom to do with students. Students within a classroom make a great authentic audience for each other, and your classroom as a group can go global and share digital creations with classes from other schools in a virtual exchange.

The Me in a Pie Chart activity can become an ideal entry point into social good and global collaboration for classrooms ready to take the leap in.

The Power of an Invitation

Melissa Collins, Elementary Teacher, Global Teacher Prize Finalist, Tennessee, USA
Twitter: @collinsnct
Instagram: drcollins1913

Any lesson in a classroom is an opportunity for global collaboration—every project, every unit, every discussion. There is always room to take your work and extend it beyond the walls of your classroom. Melissa Collins reminded me of this and of the power of invitation in a Twitter message she sent me one Friday afternoon.

2.6 Melissa Collins sent me a direct message inviting me to join her to take her project global.

Melissa Collins,PhD (National Board Fellow)
@CollinsNBCT

Hi Jennifer I have idea about a project and I need some support. I wanted to connect with you to ask how I could do it globally.Also my family lives in FLA.I was born there, too
21 Dec 2018

Melissa! Yes of course! Anything!!!
21 Dec 2018 ✓

My students are collaborating with the Civil Rights Museum in Memphis to do a peaceful demonstration march. Never done before. I want kids around the globe to make peaceful signs to address the peace SDG; however, I need a partner, maybe you if interested in how to do it using Tech. What do you think?
21 Dec 2018

Long committed to social good and advocacy and inspired by Martin Luther King Jr.'s philosophy of fighting against injustice through nonviolent, peaceful demonstrations, Melissa works daily to help children develop skills of empathy and kindness. Melissa is one of those teachers who sees every student in the world as her own. And, as she prepared to celebrate the date that would have been King's ninetieth birthday, she wanted to invite all to join in with her big idea.

In her message to me, she shared how she and her young students had partnered with the **National Civil Rights Museum** (civilrightsmuseum.org). They were creating signs of peace to lead a silent demonstration march at their school and at the museum. Recognizing that this was a unique opportunity to have students come together globally to promote peace, love, and unity for all humanity, she reached out to a few members of her Professional Learning Network to invite them to join in virtually and digitally.

Here are a few ways Melissa's team of global educators took the lesson from local to global in a matter of weeks:

- Created a simple website that outlined the steps classrooms could take to get involved: spark.adobe.com/page/e78aHOpQ4IskL/

- Invited other classrooms to create handmade and/or digital activist signs of peace. Photos and digital images added to a Padlet online board: padlet.com /JenWilliamsEdu/PeaceSigns

- Invited global classrooms to join a videoconference of a presentation by expert speakers from the National Civil Rights Museum

- Invited students to join the school march at the scheduled time and share videos of their experiences on social media using the shared hashtag #SparkEmpathy and #PeaceSignsProject

2.7 The Peace Signs Project webpage invited global classrooms to participate and was created for free with Adobe Page.

"Be a bush if you can't be a tree. If you can't be a highway, just be a trail. If you can't be a sun, be a star. For it isn't by size that you win or fail. Be the best of whatever you are." —Dr. Martin Luther King, Jr. from speech before a group of students at Barratt Junior High School in Philadelphia, October 26, 1967

By extending a personal invitation, Melissa used the power of social media and social networking to expand her classroom social good project of peace to the world. As we finished our month-long project, I asked Melissa what she felt King would say to students of today and to students participating in this project. "I believe Dr. King would tell my students that they are doing something great for humanity," she said. "They are showing the world that children can come together to create a culture of peace."

2.8 This curated page of photos and digital creations of PeaceSigns was created for free with Padlet.

2.9 Melissa's second-grade students prepare for their silent demonstration march with a class in New Jersey (third-grade teacher Michael Dunlea).

2.10 Third-grade classroom in New Jersey, USA, joining a videoconference for a presentation by experts.

2.11 Students in Melissa Collins's class march at the National Civil Rights Museum.

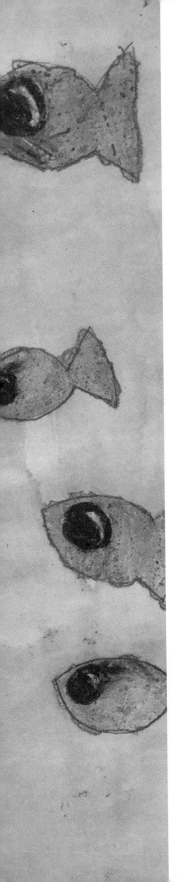

3

THE HUMAN-CENTERED LEARNING ENVIRONMENT

Our classroom spaces can support our work in social good by being responsive to students and giving them a place in which they can be fearless. Using design thinking techniques, this chapter offers ways to evaluate and optimize physical environments so that students feel welcome, safe, and supported in their endeavors and experiments.

Untitled by Grace Williams, Grade 4
Medium: Watercolor and oil pastel
Clearwater, Florida, USA

INSPIRATION: A Space Built to Make a Difference

The technology industry has a diversity problem.

In the United States in 2014, the high-tech sector was only 7% African American and 8% Hispanic—approximately half the percentage in the non-tech private sector (EEOC, 2018). Google, a company with products used in education worldwide, found even worse results in their 2016 diversity report, with data indicating an overall workforce that was 2% African American and 4% Hispanic. After two years of dedicated efforts and a companywide push for diversity, the numbers stayed mostly the same, so Google brought a team together to grapple with the problem and devise new approaches. In thinking about where to start, they worked backward until they landed on education as the key to true change.

As part of a larger strategy to create a more inclusive culture committed to improving equity and diversity, Google looked at access to technology in education, specifically for students in eighth through twelfth grades. They discovered that kids in underprivileged and under-resourced communities lacked access and exposure to computer science.

Partnering with Kurani (kurani.us), an Atlanta-based education architecture firm, they set out to create computer science spaces with access and diversity in mind. Danish Kurani, architect, founder of Kurani, and a lecturer at the Stanford School of Engineering, started the work by considering the program's objectives, then moved to thinking about how those objectives could be supported in physical space and the built environment.

In their design of the Google Code Next lab in Oakland, California, Kurani and Google worked to create a community-centric design, not in a distant location that required a commute to Silicon Valley, but right in the neighborhood of the students they wanted to reach.

3.1 This model shows the Kurani design for the Google Code Next lab in Oakland.

KURANI

"Students from Oakland should have access to tools, equipment, role models, mentors, and opportunity," Danish shared with me. The team chose a 1,500-square-foot retail storefront in the Fruitvale neighborhood, right off a public transportation train stop and nestled in between coffee shops. They then began working with local educators and neighborhood students to co-design the space.

It was important to the teams at Kurani and Google to enable students in the Oakland community to feel like they belonged in tech as much as anyone else. They wanted this group, primarily African American and Latino students, to see that the face of technology was not just Mark Zuckerberg, Bill Gates, or Elon Musk, but that it also included people like Guillermo González Camarena, the Mexican electrical engineer who invented early color television, and Melba Roy, the African-American female scientist who was part of the human computers group in NASA's Trajectory and Geodynamics Division during the 1960s.

Kurani says that for him and his team, the design challenge "was for students to see that people with the same skin and eye color as them, from neighborhoods and backgrounds like theirs, had made significant contributions to science and all our lives. And to realize that if those people belonged in the field and could have such an impact, then so can these kids. For these students, we want this to be a viable career option and something where they can say, 'This is something that I may love doing for my whole life.'"

Kurani and Google aimed to ensure that just as students may want to be the next sports star or musician, they could also see careers as computer scientists and engineers as equally "cool." They designed the learning space of the Code Next lab to work with innovative programming provided by Google to demonstrate how computer science is relevant in the students' everyday lives. They also showcased top innovations to inspire them to dream big. One wall in the lab shows an illustration of a hot-air balloon from Project Loon, one of Google's experimental initiatives from X Development (the Google-founded research and development facility and organization), which uses balloons to provide internet access to remote regions of the world. (Remember moonshots? Here they are in action!) By weaving together the past, present, and future of tech, the lab space creates a physical story and helps change the narrative for these students and, ultimately, our world.

In designing the space for the Code Next lab, Kurani and Google wanted to create a learning environment that encouraged students to be confident and courageous and free from perfectionism. The space was designed to invite experimentation and exploration, with kids encouraged to tinker and play. They incorporated concepts of iteration into the architecture, and critical actions of peer review and feedback into the walls and displays.

Space, paired with pedagogy, offers these students a new type of hands-on, project-based learning (PBL). In the Code Next lab, students can get into a mindset to think like a maker. And the teams at Kurani and Google wanted students to explore not only with their hands but also with their minds. Thoughtful building and design techniques expose how space works, how things move, and how pieces all fit together to form a functioning whole. With computer science as a "cool" opportunity within reach, students could start to see where they themselves fit into it all—as needed and valued parts of the whole.

The Code Next lab is now up and running in Fruitvale, and it has already had an impact on learning and social good in the community. Research by Kurani (2018) showed:

- Access to computer science had increased from 50% to 100% for students in the community.

- 97% of students reported feeling the lab provided more opportunities for hands-on learning than traditional school spaces.

- Two out of three students said the space made them feel like they could change the world.

- 80% of students said that the lab space had given them the confidence to pursue a career in computer science or technology.

Google, Kurani, and others in computer science and technology look to education as the starting point for addressing inequities and diversity issues in the next generation of tech leaders. We as educators can also look to them and to their advances in architecture and design of space to help us to better support high-quality learning for everyone, everywhere.

LEARNING SPACE DESIGN: STUDENTS AT THE CENTER

My own interest in learning space design stems from my early teaching and research work in the flexible spaces of Montessori schools. My experience of being in classrooms with rows of desks with a teacher at the front pretty much ended the day I graduated from college. Recognizing the impact the physical environment had on learning in Montessori schools, I was able to see how the classroom—including the furniture, the resources and materials, the participants, the arrangement, and the culture—is key. I found that supportive spaces developed through the lens of empathy and amplification of student voice can inspire new ways of thinking and working for students.

For more than one hundred years, Montessori classrooms have allowed freedom in movement and choice of activity with purposeful spaces for quiet work, group work, and hands-on learning. In the early 1900s, when Maria Montessori was developing her innovative classrooms, hers were the exception. Fast forward 120 years—and this type of classroom is still the exception. But things are starting to change.

Instructional practice is dramatically shifting, and schools are finding the traditional designs of classrooms—from the shapes of rooms to heights of ceilings to the need for natural light, power outlets, and controlled temperatures—need to be reimagined to better support the use of emerging technologies and innovations in thinking and doing. Traditional classrooms with teacher-centered pedagogies and students-as-recipients-of-information models no longer fit.

Schools with new types of learning spaces, like the classrooms in the Code Next lab, support critical thinking, problem-solving, and collaboration, and they also show potential to reflect culture, diversity, social-emotional learning, and social good.

By optimizing physical and virtual spaces, we can reconfigure the conversation and bring the students and all that they represent to the center. And to enable learning to happen anywhere for everyone, we need to start by looking not at the furniture, but at our people.

EDUCATION, MEET USER EXPERIENCE

If, for a moment, we think of a classroom as if it were a product, we can begin to understand how design can impact student engagement and learning. User experience, a fundamental component of design in edtech, seeks to better understand a person's perceptions and responses when they use a product, service, or system (ISO, 2009). A user's actions, duration of use, or even number of clicks on a website page can be assessed through interviews, surveys, or observation. This data informs design decisions, so the user reaction influences future versions of the product.

By applying user experience to education, we can prioritize the feelings, motivations, and values of our users—"users" for us being our students. Our "service," then, is teaching, and our "package" of the classroom contains a lot of "features." We have furniture, instructional materials, resources, lighting, flooring, textures, temperature, air quality, and on and on. For students, the experience of learning starts the minute they walk into the classroom, even before we bring instruction into the conversation. Students bring their own experiences, backgrounds, and expectations into the classroom space, and we as teachers need to be consciously aware there is an immediate interaction or exchange between student and space.

Though certain elements may be out of our control (furniture provided by the school, number of windows, number of devices, and so on), we certainly can help shape the way our students feel. Do they feel welcome, safe, and wanted each day? Are we making sure by asking them?

User experience in classroom design can be as simple as us checking in: "How does the temperature feel for you?" "Are you able to hear when you sit in the back?" "How might we make our classroom more comfortable for you?"

A message of "I see you, I am happy you are here, and you matter to me" can make all the difference for a child who is unsure if the world is taking notice.

Here are some other quick (and free) ways to incorporate user experience and student-centered practices into space design decisions:

- Interview students and have them tell you about spaces (on campus and/or outside of school) where they enjoy spending time. Use guiding questions to help pinpoint areas that evoke positive emotions, then get more information to help determine the causes of those emotions. Consider sharing questions in a **Google Form** (google.com/forms) to capture and record all responses.

- Make subtle changes to the classroom space and survey students quantitatively with Likert five-point scales or qualitatively by asking them to share one word that describes how the change makes them feel. Be sure to record over time.

- Observe and note areas or activities that students self-select when given a choice.

ACCESS: FIRST AND ALWAYS

Access must come first. Always. In all planning, implementation, and assessment discussions in education, access must be at the top of the list of agenda items and talking points. All learning experiences must be accessible to all learners. As teachers, we must be sensitive and mindful of the individual learning needs of all students, including English language learners, students with learning differences, and students from economically disadvantaged homes or rural communities.

Professional builders and architects like Kurani incorporate accessibility into designs from the start. Universal access for all is regulated into constructions—from ramps for entry to positions and heights of door handles and elevator buttons to noise levels, lighting levels, and Braille and audio options. All users are considered.

Learning from these other professions, how might we do better at this in education? Here are a few starting points:

- Consider the physical needs of your students: (1) chair sizes, (2) table heights, (3) lighting, (4) acoustics, and (5) mobility.

- Put yourself in your students' seats—literally. Is there a relationship between seat location and access to information? Does one classroom area provide a different experience in terms of sound, sight, or temperature?

- Be mindful of the home-school connection and of assigning work for home that requires Wi-Fi when internet may not be available or reliable.

DEFINE LEARNING ZONES

KURANI

3.2 Students work in different learning zones at the Google Code Next lab.

Tech-supported instruction allows teachers to be untethered from a desk and away from the front of the room so they can extend learning to all areas of the classroom. Defined learning zones within a classroom space can provide intention and purpose to guide different learning activities—lecture areas for demonstrations, collaborative spaces for group work, and individual computer stations for self-directed work. Give students agency and choice in their ability to customize their environments and match workspaces to learning goals.

LEARNING TODAY IS ON THE MOVE. Encourage the use of mobile devices to decentralize learning from traditional computer science labs and computer science classes, and instead explore hallways, nooks, outdoor spaces, and virtual spaces to extend learning and experience.

TAKE BRAINSTORM WALKS. Harness the power of movement and its ability to fuel the brain and facilitate new, creative thought. Students can record ideas with tech (talk-to-text, photos, audio recordings) or with notebooks.

BUILD A COLLABORATION STATION. Push a table against a wall, add a screen with video capability, and invite students to gather around on stools. Collaboration stations can be used for small group sharing sessions with mirroring of devices or for small group virtual exchange experiences.

3.3 Students can change the space based on purpose and learning objectives.

SPACES THAT REFLECT AND CELEBRATE DIVERSITY

Remember that you and your students are part of the classroom's environment. You together create the culture. You together create the community. You together create the conditions for members of the classroom to feel comfortable, confident, and valued. Learning space design is more than just paint color. We need to move conversations away from rolling chairs and expensive furniture. The architecture of learning is how we use the space we enter. It is the words we say and how we make people feel.

As demonstrated by the research Kurani and Google conducted in the Code Next lab, the messages our students hear and see influence their understanding of self and of opportunity. Our classroom spaces can help us break down systemic barriers faced by our students and community members as we ensure our students see themselves reflected in the space and in the learning resources.

With intentionality in the decisions we make and the words we use, we can better support all students—most specifically our students from underrepresented groups. Below are some tips for how to support your students with intention.

- Understand and voice your own unconscious biases and take conscious action on them.

- Call students by their preferred names and gender pronouns. If you are unsure, ask.

- Resist breaking working groups into boys vs. girls.

- Review instructional materials (books, presentation slides, resources) and ensure that diversity in race and gender are represented in images and with names used in examples. Avoid stock photos or worksheets that use stereotypical roles, images, or names (e.g., male engineer, female nurse, boy named Joe, girl named Sally).

- Check in with your students privately and ask if they feel adequately and fairly represented in the space and in instruction.

- Use your walls to reflect the community and students you serve. Look to the walls of the Code Next lab that showcased and celebrated computer scientists and inventors from minority groups. Invite your students to take part in researching and selecting the individuals to be incorporated into wall displays.

3.4 Guillermo González Camarena, Mexican engineer and inventor, is showcased in the Google Code Next lab.

Influential Computer Scientists, Engineers, and Inventors Representative of Minority Groups

Gerald "Jerry" Lawson, Engineer

Jerry Lawson created the first video game console with interchangeable cartridges. His invention, the first home console of its kind, and his related work in the mid-1970s paved the way for future home gaming systems. He was honored for his innovative work by the International Game Developers Association (igda. org) in March 2011, one month before he died.

Kimberly Bryant, Electrical Engineer and Founder of Black Girls Code

Kimberly Bryant created Black Girls Code (blackgirlscode.com) in 2011 to help young girls of color learn computer coding and programming languages such as Scratch and Ruby on Rails. Aiming to increase the number of African American women in technology and STEM careers, she is set on training one million girls of color through classes and programs by the year 2040.

Victor Celorio, Inventor

Victor Celorio is the president of InstaBook Corporation and creator of the InstaBook Maker technology, which supports the making of print-on-demand books. Born in Mexico City, he now lives in Florida and has been granted multiple U.S. patents for his inventions.

Sandra Begay-Campbell, Civil and Structural Engineer

Sandra Begay-Campbell is the head of the Tribal Energy Program at the Sandia National Laboratories in New Mexico. Her work on photovoltaics has helped bring solar power to remote Navajo villages.

continued

continued

Mark Dean, Computer Scientist, Engineer, and Inventor

Mark Dean led a team of engineers at IBM and holds three of the company's original nine patents. He is credited with helping to invent the color PC monitor, the first gigahertz chip able to do one billion calculations per second, and the Industry Standard Architecture (ISA) system bus (a system that allows disk drives, printers, and monitors to plug directly into computers). His name is associated with more than twenty patents.

Donna Auguste, Engineer and Inventor

In her role as a senior engineering manager at Apple, Donna Auguste developed the Newton Personal Digital Assistant (PDA), a technology that informed the design of the iPhone. After leaving Apple, she started Freshwater Software, which sold in 2001 for $107,000,000, and she then founded the Leave a Little Room Foundation, a nonprofit that helps provide housing, electricity, and vaccinations to underprivileged communities around the world.

Marc Hannah, Computer Scientist

Marc Hannah co-founded Silicon Graphics, Inc. (SGI), a manufacturer of high-performance computer hardware and software. SGI technology was used to create cutting-edge visual effects for films such as *Jurassic Park* and *Terminator 2*. After leaving SGI, Hannah went on to work with other tech teams and helped create the MP3 player for Game Boy Advance.

Timnit Gebru, AI Researcher

As a researcher at Microsoft Research and now at Google, Timnit Gebru has worked to examine the ethical and moral implications of artificial intelligence. She worked with a team to develop a machine learning algorithm that used Google Street View images of cars to predict census data such as income, carbon emissions, and crime rates. She is the founder of Black in AI (blackinai.github.io) and is committed to eliminating racial biases in AI systems.

CONNECT TO INTERESTS TO BUILD RELEVANCY

If we truly want to connect to the hearts and minds of all our students, we need to go beyond boxed curricula, textbooks, and rows of desks. We need to move away from passively accepting conditions as they are. And we need to question and reinvent and move around the pieces of our classrooms until we find approaches that fit for all. The time spent working to uncover the interests and passions of our students is worth it—*they* are worth it. The student—with all the things she or he represents, loves, and hopes for—must be at the heart of our rooms and our teaching.

- Build time into the schedule to get to know your students. Be explicit—mark your lesson plan or calendar as "Discover the interests and passions of my students." Remember to dedicate time to the things you value.

- Draw lines of connection from student passions to the way things work. Consider the wall display of the deconstructed Beats headphones in the Google Code Next lab. Take things apart, add labels, inspire questions (**Figure 3.5**).

- Use your classroom spaces to tell the history of technologies that relate to your students and their lives. Look to the interactive display in the Oakland lab of video game controllers from the 1980s and how those lay the groundwork for the way computer scientists now shape how people game (**Figure 3.5**).

- *Show* your students that you hear them. Visually connect their passions to education and learning. The graphic of the soccer player Neymar on the wall of the Code Next lab shows students how he uses sensors on his soccer balls to train and track performance—the intersection of technology and sports (**Figure 3.5**).

3.5 Displays and images can connect computer science and tech to student interests.

ROOM FOR GROWTH

Human-centered learning spaces, infused with technology and innovative practice, can make static, sterile environments come alive with activity, inquiry, and cooperative learning. Dynamic spaces become part of the learning experience, with the walls, windows, floors, and displays all helping move ideas forward. As ideas advance and education morphs and changes, we need rooms flexible enough to pivot and develop. Here are five key classroom design elements to prepare learning spaces for bold teaching and learning.

Make Ideas Visible

As technology-rich school programs make dedicated efforts to move learning from passive to active, there is an increased need to make learning and thinking visible. Prepared environments can allow for transparency of thought and encourage students to document their learning in relevant ways. With the use of devices and software in instruction, ideas must not be locked down in hard-to-access places. Classrooms can serve as extensions of ideas: all spaces can be learning spaces for displaying understanding and creative thought with writing surfaces on walls, tables, and windows. Mobile writing spaces, such as small whiteboards, chalkboards, clipboards, sticky notes, and chart paper, can offer space for brainstorming and ideation.

Digital spaces can offer areas for concept mapping and collaborative thought, allowing for ease of use and participation for all. My favorite tech tools for ideation and mind mapping include **Stickies.io** (stickies.io), **Popplet** (popplet.com), **Flipgrid** (flipgrid.com), and **Padlet** (padlet.com). For project management and flow, my favorites that I use daily are **Trello** (trello.com) and **Slack** (slack.com).

Consider displays. Repurpose the time you would typically dedicate to making bulletin boards yourself and instead allow your students to create the boards. Create room for generating possibilities and celebrating the process of learning rather than showcasing only the final products of learning. Consider displaying failed attempts or works-in-progress as opposed to the shiny, polished outcomes. Let students know through your actions that trial-and-error and experimentation are encouraged—and that life is messy and not always a snapshot of perfection. Often, the most interesting parts are in the backstory.

Digital and Analog Harmony

Learning space design is a key factor when seeking the best balance between high-tech and low-tech resources. With a well-planned design, digital tools and analog tools can work in parallel, and multiple modes of learning can be incorporated to support all students.

To accommodate a range of tools and practices, classroom spaces can be outfitted with large worktables, ample floor space, and areas for recording and production. Students can mirror devices to wall-mounted monitors to make it easier to work together in both physical and virtual environments. By using digital and non-digital tools in tandem, students can accelerate and deepen experience. In the case of social good, spaces such as these can help our kids make personal connections to concepts, understand how distinct parts can fit into a whole, and meaningfully identify patterns of their worlds.

It's More Than Furniture and More Than Paint Color

Moving beyond decoration, how can we prioritize building healthy spaces that are safe and supportive, with clean air, comfortable temperatures, proper lighting and acoustics, as well as access to outdoor spaces and resources such as reliable Wi-Fi, power for charging, and working technology?

"Teaching boldly" means we must also think pedagogically. Instructional decisions must be grounded in strong instructional design. Choice of new wall colors must be connected to evidence of impact, as opposed to being based on what subjectively seems "cute" or "fun" or "Pinterest-worthy." Additionally, flexible furniture alone does not equate to changed practice. Chairs and tables on casters can be beneficial, but we as teachers need to understand why and be able to articulate the benefits for our students (and for ourselves as educators). It will be important for us to resist the latest "buzz" idea until we confirm the data and that supportive research behind it exists.

Makerspaces

To learn about makerspaces, I went to a top makerspace expert, Laura Fleming (@LFlemingEdu). Committed to supporting play, tinkering, inquiry, and open-ended exploration for all, Laura has worked with schools around the world to design custom makerspaces. "While anyone can create a makerspace, there are critical attributes that set apart makerspaces and GREAT maker-spaces," Laura told me. The following seven attributes of GREAT makerspaces, according to Laura, allow for the creation of powerful learning experiences:

1. Personalized

2. Deep

3. Empowering

4. Equitable

5. Differentiated

6. Intentional

7. Inspiring

Your makerspace design process must include proper planning with connection to data about your students, your school community, and the wider world. You want to build a makerspace that is unique to your community ("no two maker-spaces should be alike") and sustainable (Fleming, 2019).

One of Laura's top makerspace tips: it cannot be about the "stuff." Though many people associate the maker movement with items such as 3D printers and laser cutters, the supplies should be determined after themes are uncovered and in place. Laura shared her "Worlds of Making 'MAKER' Framework" to help guide the selection of products for your makerspace.

M: Mobility

Does the product support free-range learning and liberate learners from the limitations of a physical makerspace, therefore increasing equity and access?

A: Allows for Open-Ended Exploration

Is the product limited to step-by-step directions, or does it maximize inquiry by allowing the opportunity for open-ended explorations?

K: Knowledge of Student Needs, Wants, and Interests

Do you understand your learners? Does the product connect to the needs, wants, and interests of your students?

E: Empowerment and Engagement

Does the product empower *all* students by meeting them where they are? Does it have a low barrier of entry for engagement?

R: Relevance

Does the product have relevance to your school community and/or global trends and best practices?

To learn more about makerspaces, the maker movement, and Laura's work with global classrooms, check out these resources:

- *The Kickstart Guide to Making GREAT Makerspaces* (Fleming, Corwin, 2018)

- *World of Making: Best Practices for Establishing a Makerspace for your School* (Fleming, Corwin, 2015)

- Worlds of Making Annual Top 10 Makerspace Favorites: worldsofmaking. com/makerspace-favorites

Be Prepared for Change

Classroom spaces cannot and should not ever really be "done." Classrooms need to be adaptable and ready for change so they can reflect the people in the space and the technologies and innovative practices that fill the rooms. Just as our world evolves, our rooms must as well.

Change will likely come in two primary forms: incremental change and large-scale change. First, we should anticipate (and welcome) the need to make modifications to spaces incrementally throughout the school year. As we move from one instructional unit to the next, as a new student joins the class, as an unanticipated world or personal event occurs, our rooms too should evolve and develop. We also need to respond to large-scale change. A new school year can bring new students, new policies, new initiatives, new demands, and in some cases, even entirely new roles. Classroom environments need to be considered, with adjustments made as part of implementation plans.

Changed spaces change practice, and changed practice opens up new ways students can interact with each other and with new information. Change will come; we need to be ready to change with it and adjust expectations.

Black Girls Code Lab

Working to increase the number of women of color in technology roles, Black Girls Code is committed to providing girls from underrepresented communities access to technology and computer science skills. The nonprofit organization was founded in 2011 and has reached more than 8,000 young women through its work in fourteen worldwide chapters. In efforts to offer positive and meaningful experiences with technology to girls in New York City, Black Girls Code partnered with Danish Kurani to build a custom Black Girls Code lab housed in Google's New York City office. The project, bringing together two impact-driven organizations, was designed not only to demystify technology but also to empower the next generation of women and tech leaders.

As with the Google Code Next lab, Kurani transformed a space and showed how design can reshape the future of learning. "Architecture should be leveraged to make the world a better place. It should improve the environment, it should improve the lives of people, it should help solve some of the world's largest and most daunting problems," Danish shared.

As an immigrant to the U.S., Danish understands the social mobility that comes from being educated. When considering where we are as a society, he says, "education is the most proactive thing we can do." And, in the case of the Black Girls Code lab, the space is used to directly address social inequities we face as a world:

> So, the first thing to establish is that design has a profound impact on our lives, as does the design of the built environment that we occupy on a daily basis. This means where we live, where we work, where we play, where we go to school, where we recreate, all of these places that are key aspects of our lived experience are designed by someone, and the design of those experiences plays a great role in how we feel, what we are able to accomplish, and possibly even what we think while we are in those spaces.

> As we take the built environment of schools—the learning environment—there is a strong link between the design and the way that students and teachers can perform in that space. And that performance is tied to many factors that we look at. It is the totality of the physical learning environment. As we design and

curate the experience, all the aspects of the environment are geared toward optimizing the chances that a student can learn and learn well and that a teacher can teach and teach well.

The Black Girls Code lab is outfitted with cutting-edge technology, including virtual reality stations, deconstructed computers, and circuit boards lining the walls. Girls are invited to join workshops, hackathons, classes, and even parent-daughter events. The space is designed to both *support* the learning and *be* the learning, with an x-ray wall installation that gamifies the space to encourage girls to explore the outer facades and inner workings of common tech products, such as iPhones. With sliding panels, the girls can find matches between parts and see relationships between what is visible on the surface of products and what lies inside and controls the devices.

Though there is not a quick fix to the tech industry's gaps in terms of diversity and inclusion, programs like Black Girls Code and spaces like the Black Girls Code lab are starting points to help build confidence and skills with students from under-represented groups. Visit blackgirlscode.com to learn more about Black Girls Code and the Black Girls Code lab in New York City.

3.6 Black Girls Code lab in New York City, designed by Danish Kurani.

TAKE ACTION
START LOCAL TO GO GLOBAL

Take action on going beyond the walls of your learning space into your local community. Seek out a local museum, park, organization, or business that aligns to ways your class is taking action on social good. Access online resources, plan for an expert representative to visit the class (either in person or virtually), or set up a field trip to visit and learn. Here are four museums centered on social good that welcome virtual visitors:

- **NATIONAL CENTER FOR CIVIL AND HUMAN RIGHTS**
  Atlanta, Georgia, USA: civilandhumanrights.org

- **UNITED STATES HOLOCAUST MEMORIAL MUSEUM**
  Washington, D.C., USA: ushmm.org

- **MUSEUM OF TOLERANCE**
  Los Angeles, California, USA: museumoftolerance.com

- **MUSEUM FOR THE UNITED NATIONS—UN LIVE**
  Copenhagen, Denmark: unlivemuseum.org

BOLD INVITATION
THE WORLD IS YOUR CLASSROOM

Teachers who view the world as their classroom see all students of the world as their own. They understand that for the success and strength of one, there must be success and strength for all. As you aspire to flatten the walls of your classroom and bring the world to your students and your students to the world, consider leading a schoolwide virtual exchange project.

Use virtual exchange tools such as Empatico (elementary) and Skype, Zoom, or Google Hangouts (all grades) to connect your students to others around the world and then share your experiences with administrators, colleagues, and classroom parents. Bulletin boards or wall spaces in school hallways or in the front offices can become interactive spaces that show the connections being created.

One of my favorite examples of this was from Kathi Kersznowski (@Kerszi), a technology integration specialist in New Jersey. For a virtual exchange initiative she led for six schools in her district, she worked with classrooms to design interactive bulletin boards that showed all the global connections made through virtual exchanges during the school year. Students who passed by could see connections develop and were encouraged to engage in their own exchanges to add to the boards (**Figures 3.7**).

KATHI KERZNOWSKI

3.7 Kathi Kersznowski worked with classrooms to design interactive bulletin boards that showed global connections made through virtual exchanges.

MY PEACEMAKER PROFILE ACTIVITY #3
MAPPING A LEARNING SPACE

Space design, guided by conscious and committed observation and sustained user feedback, can be a powerful tool in the process of teaching boldly and reimagining learning. As you take action on creating spaces that are representative of your learners and responsive to the world around you, space mapping exercises can provide the data points and insights you need to guide your decision-making.

Space mapping can be done at any point in the school year and is most powerful when repeated and used over time. It is a useful practice to provide understanding of any behavior or circumstance a teacher would like to measure, such as analyzing class schedules, assessing a single student's routine, and evaluating efficiency and impact of a component of instruction or learning.

Here, our variables will be engagement and expression of representativeness in the space at the classroom level. The analysis can also be done for a campus space (e.g., cafeteria, playground, school bus), the entire school, or the community (e.g., school-to-home).

STEP 1: Create an illustrated map of your classroom.

You can sketch the space using tech tools, you can draw your classroom using pencil and paper, or you can copy the template (available at jenwilliamsedu. com/peacemaker-profile.html). All you need is a general view of the room (e.g., walls, shelves, tables). If you are using a digital diagram, duplicate or clone the image. If you are using a paper diagram, be sure to make printed copies.

Learning Space Engagement Mapping

Classroom _____

Activity _____

Date/Time _____

Students Observed:

3.8 You can use a paper diagram to analyze your students' use of the classroom.

STEP 2: Determine your observation times.

With your learning space diagram in hand, block off several points in the schedule of the day to observe student activity. You can observe one student, several students, or the entire class. For example:

OBSERVATION BLOCK 1: Morning work time / 30 minutes / Students A, B, C

OBSERVATION BLOCK 2: Choice time / 45 minutes / Students A, B, C

OBSERVATION BLOCK 3: Technology block / 25 minutes / Students A, B, C

Note: Ensure you are not assigning students to specific spaces during the times that you're observing them. These need to be times where students have freedom of movement and choice of activity. If you have not done formal observations of your classroom in the past, you will want to prepare your students by letting them know that for those blocks of time you will not be available to conference with them or answer questions at length.

STEP 3: Map student engagement within the space.

During the observation, map student activity according to selected spaces. If you are observing all students or a single student, you can simply mark activity in the space (where in the classroom are they are self-selecting to work?) with a black dot on the diagram. If you are observing a small group of students, you can denote each student by mapping each one with a different color (e.g., Student A: blue, Student B: green, Student C: purple). Repeat this process with a new, unmarked diagram for your next set of observations.

STEP 4: Obtain feedback from the students.

For this activity, you will need to block off approximately forty-five minutes in your schedule. You will gather all your students together and ask them to offer their opinions and feelings on the space. Here is a sample script and flow:

1. Students, as we have discussed, I view our classroom as your classroom. This is your space for learning, and I want to ensure that you feel that you—your interests, your culture, your hopes and dreams—are reflected in the classroom.

2. Today, we are going to sketch out our classroom and mark places that we feel are mirrors of us. Let me show you how we can do this using me (*you as the teacher*) as an example.

3. Watch as I sketch out the room (*use easel paper, a whiteboard, or a mirrored image from your device*). See how I am adding in the bookshelves, the tables, and the doors.

4. Now, I am going to circle places in the room to answer these two questions:

   • Where are places in the room I feel I can be creative?

   • Where are places in the room I feel reflect me, my interests, my culture, and my hopes and dreams?

   See how here I circle the makerspace because I like to build and create there. I also will circle this framed painting of the scientist Jane Goodall with her chimpanzees in Africa, because she loves animals and believes in helping the environment like me. I am going to make notes about those, too (*make notes on diagram: makerspace = space to create and build; Goodall = she loves animals and the environment like me*).

5. Now, I would like for each of you to make a diagram of our room. (*Use tech tools or pencil/paper.*) Let's take ten minutes for each of you to sketch your diagram of the classroom. Stop after you draw the classroom, and then I will tell you the next step.

6. Let's come back together now. I will write the first question on the board here for us:

   • Where are places in the room where I feel I can be creative?

   I would like you to think about our room and then circle a spot in the room where you feel you can be creative. I picked the makerspace, but you can pick anywhere. Circle that space and make a simple note. (*Invite a few students to share responses.*)

7. For our second question, I want you to think about an area of the room that you feel is representative of you—your interests, your culture, your hopes and dreams.

- Where are places in the room I feel represent me?

You can circle a place or places and make a quick note of what and why. (*Invite a few students to share responses.*)

8. *Depending on the age of the students, you can now facilitate a discussion with students to get their feedback on ways the current space could be changed or improved to (1) encourage creativity and (2) better reflect the students in the room. You can make an anchor chart to capture responses. Be sure to note any anecdotes or student comments for your own records.*

9. Thank you for your feedback today. Let's keep thinking together on ways we can use our classroom to support our learning. If you think of anything later today or later in the week, please let me know!

STEP 5: Analyze the data. Create an action plan.

Triangulate the data you have obtained. Search for themes as you analyze (1) the learning space maps, (2) the student diagrams, and (3) noted student anecdotes or comments (**Figure 3.16**). What are areas for improvement? What are specific actions you can take to demonstrate to students that you heard them, you see them, and you are responding by changing the space?

Free and Simple Sketching Tools for Devices

Amber McCormick (@EdtechAmber), educator and sketchnoter, recommends these tech tools for sketching:

- Microsoft devices: SketchPad in the Ink Workspace

- Apple devices: Sketching tools in Notes

- iPhone and iPad: Paper by WeTransfer (paper.bywetransfer.com)

Learning Space Engagement Mapping

Analysis of engagement in relation to creativity and representation within classroom

Teacher: _____

Class: _____

Date: _____

Themes, noted reflections, and areas for improvement	Specific actions based on analysis (with timeline)

3.9 This is an example of how you can use a diagram to map your classroom space.

lee
2·25·19

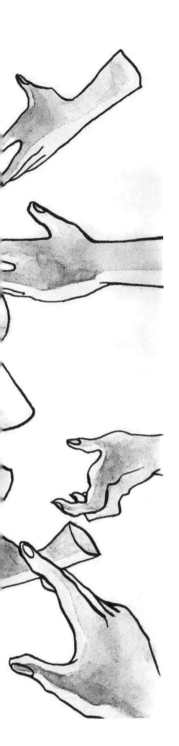

4

SHARING STORIES TO OFFER PANORAMA

Storytelling is one of the most powerful tools that students can use to share their messages of social change. In this chapter, you'll learn how we as educators can transform our students from consumers of content to creators of content by introducing them to many forms of narrative and giving them a broad range of tools to express their ideas.

Breaking Free by Lee Patel, Grade 12
Medium: India ink and watercolor
Teacher: Estella Owoimaha-Church, English and Theater Teacher
Inglewood, California, USA

INSPIRATION: The Story of the Rules of the Story

Storytelling is an art form. A good storyteller not only offers a compelling story but also—and perhaps even more importantly—connects powerfully to the human spirit.

In 2011, then-Pixar (and now Google) storyboard artist Emma Coats (@lawnrocket) posted a series of tweets in which she shared twenty-two rules of storytelling. Offered as nuggets of wisdom that the world could explore, analyze, and treasure, the ideas gave artists, digital creators, writers, and learners a glimpse into the genius behind some of the best stories of our time. The tweets were a micro-storytelling adventure for all to enjoy; people followed along online as the story of the rules unfolded.

4.1 This was the first tweet in Emma Coats's series of rules of storytelling.

1. You admire a character for trying more than for their successes.

2. Keep in mind what's interesting to you as an audience, not what's fun to do as a writer. They can be very different.

3. Trying for theme is important, but you won't see what the story is actually about until you're at the end of it. Now rewrite.

4. Once upon a time there was _____.
   Every day, _____.
   One day _____.
   Because of that, _____.
   Because of that, _____.
   Until finally _____.

5. Simplify. Focus. Combine characters. Hop over detours. You'll feel like you're losing valuable stuff but it sets you free.

6. What is your character good at, comfortable with? Throw the opposite at them. Challenge them. How do they deal?

7. Come up with your ending before you figure out your middle. Endings are hard, get yours working up front.

8. Finish your story, let go even if it's not perfect. In an ideal world you have both, but move on. Do better next time.

9. When you're stuck, make a list of what wouldn't happen next. Lots of times the material to get you unstuck will show up.

10. Pull apart the stories you like. What you like in them is a part of you; you've got to recognize it before you can use it.

11. Putting it on paper lets you start fixing it. If it stays in your head, a perfect idea, you'll never share it with anyone.

12. Discount the first thing that comes to mind—and the second, third, fourth and fifth. Get the obvious out of the way. Surprise yourself.

13. Give your characters opinions. Passive/malleable might seem likable to you as you write, but it's poison to the audience.

14. Why must you tell this story? What's the belief burning within you that your story feeds off of? That's the heart of it.

15. **If you were your character, in this situation, how would you feel?** Honesty lends credibility to unbelievable situations.

16. **What are the stakes?** Give us reason to root for the character. What happens if they don't succeed? Stack the odds against.

17. **No work is ever wasted.** If it's not working, let go and move on. It'll come back around to be useful later.

18. **You have to know yourself:** the difference between doing your best and fussing. Story is testing, not refining.

19. **Coincidences to get characters into trouble are great;** coincidences to get them out of it are cheating.

20. **Exercise:** Take the building blocks of a movie you dislike. How do you rearrange them into what you do like?

21. **You must identify with your situation and/or characters;** you can't just write "cool." What would make you act that way?

22. **What's the essence of your story?** The most economical telling of it? If you know that, you can build out from there.

Later expanded into a blog series by Coats, the list was then made into an ebook by her former Pixar colleague, Stephan Vladimir Bugaj (@stephanbugaj). The book, titled *Pixar's 22 Rules of Story (that aren't really Pixar's): Analyzed* (Bugaj, 2013), is available as a free download and offers musings and insight on each of the points of Coat's twenty-two tweets.

This story, about twenty-two fantastic tips on the art of storytelling, also serves as an excellent model of digital storytelling: one person with expertise and wisdom using a social medium to share ideas with the world. Simple tweets, leading to blog posts, leading to application and adaptation. That makes for a great story!

BETWEEN PURPOSE AND PERSPECTIVE, SITS THE STORY

Our hyper-connected world of technology can provide pathways for sharing and tools for powerful storytelling. Genius that years ago would have been sealed in tall office buildings behind locked doors can now be shared, as demonstrated by the story about the twenty-two rules of storytelling that were presented in a connected monologue as an open invitation to explore, expand, and learn. Today we are seeing individual viewpoints offered organically through quick on-the-go livestreamed stories and through shared ideas synthesized into short video talks as popularized by TED Talks and TEDx.

As educators, we have a responsibility to guide students as they become illustrators of the human experience—stewards of truth and accuracy—and to help them incorporate the new while preserving the aesthetic whole. We need to help students filter the sometimes noisy spaces of technology and innovation. We need to ensure that the richness of humanity is protected and that the stories that sit between purpose and perspective are told and contextualized.

STUDENTS AS CREATORS AND CREATIVE PROBLEM SOLVERS

As our students come to understand their own connections to purpose, technology can amplify and spread their messages and stories so that they cross over content areas and move beyond classroom walls. In developing a plan to support your students as storytellers, ask yourself these questions:

- With increased interdependence and globalization, how can I best bring stories of the world to my students, and my students' stories to the world?

- How can I extend the perspective of my students so they can address problems and issues through the lens of an integrated worldview as opposed to a collection of independent skills?

- Are my classrooms isolated "docks," or are we building bridges with other classrooms around the world?

Accelerated technology adoption in schools allows for meaningful use of web-based tools and apps for learning through storytelling and global collaboration. Paired with innovative teaching practices and advanced methodologies, the use of technology can empower students to investigate and interact with the world beyond their immediate environments.

Teachers who want to incorporate global projects into their lessons have a wide variety of productivity and creativity applications available. As with any lesson design, the choice of tools needs to be based on the essential aim of the learning. The following three questions are offered as starting points for story-telling/media literacy lessons.

Power of Stories and Perspective

ESSENTIAL QUESTION: *How can students share stories with authentic and diverse audiences? How can students demonstrate their capacities to recognize the perspectives of others and celebrate geographic, linguistic, and cultural differences?*

PEDAGOGICAL BASIS: Standards of practice call for students to communicate with diverse populations across the four primary areas of communication: reading, writing, speaking, and listening. Purposeful conversations and sharing of stories allow for the exchange of ideas and personal narratives. Shared experience can therefore lead to empathy and an awareness of the world and how it works.

Reason with Evidence

ESSENTIAL QUESTION: *How does student work illustrate an ability to investigate the world and matters of global significance?*

PEDAGOGICAL BASIS: As part of a collaborative team, students today must possess the ability to ask and explore critical and researchable questions.

Investigations, informed by disciplinary and interdisciplinary origins, should follow a structure that engages team members to work together to identify patterns, generate possibilities, and explore alternate solutions.

Creation of Content

ESSENTIAL QUESTION: *How can students as creators of content produce digital artifacts that represent creative problem-solving and/or understanding of concepts?*

PEDAGOGICAL BASIS: Students should demonstrate the ability to construct knowledge and deep understanding of the world. With a focus on big ideas and central themes, students can work together to create and propel learning forward through active engagement and visible thinking routines. Students as content creators and global collaborators have the power to make digital artifacts that can serve as representations of understanding and shared experience.

TED Talks

TED Talk and TEDx videos can be a great way to get your students considering alternative viewpoints and presentation styles. TED Talk videos that I love to share with students when thinking about storytelling and creative thinking include:

- **"The Danger of the Single Story"** TED Talk by Chimamanda Ngozi Adichie (bit.ly/2XUoa63)

- **"The Writer's Block"** TEDxKids@SMU Talk by Asha Christensen (bit.ly/2StUOAg)

- **"What If You Could Trade a Paperclip for a House?"** TEDx Talk by Kyle MacDonald (bit.ly/2O8VpOs)

Leveraging Digital Tools

Digital storytelling, or using digital tools to tell a story, opens up creative possibilities for our students. Monica Burns, educator, founder of Class Tech Tips (@ClassTechTips and classtechtips.com), and author of multiple books, has been a pioneering educator in the space of digital storytelling and the use of edtech tools for learning. In a 2018 interview, she shared some of her thoughts with me:

What are your thoughts on the importance of digital storytelling in classrooms today?

Digital storytelling is more than "once upon a time," but preparing students to share their thoughts, ideas, and questions in a multimedia format. This type of communication skill is essential for students of all ages as they work to combine images, text, music, and voice to share their learning. Digital storytelling provides an opportunity for students to shift from their all too common roles as content consumers to the creators of content in multiple formats.

How do you see students taking action for our world? What powerful stories have stuck with you?

Students today understand the power of leveraging social channels for impact. They realize that a compelling story can captivate the attention of the world—even for a short period of time. When students share their experiences and desire to effect change, it is hard to turn away. One of the most powerful examples of this has been the way the students at Stoneman Douglas High School leveraged digital channels to make sure their voices were heard following the devastating school shooting at their campus.

What do you see as the role of technology in storytelling?

Technology can help level the playing field for storytellers. It makes it easier than ever to create captivating content that will grab and hold the attention of the audience. The access to music, visuals, and editing tools that now live on smartphones and tablets can help more people tell their stories.

What are ways educators can find the intersections of digital storytelling, digital citizenship, and social good?

I'm a big fan of the Adobe Spark tools. Ben Forta and I recently co-authored a book, 40 Ways to Inject Creativity into Your Classroom with Adobe Spark (2018). I love how students can quickly and easily create powerful stories to share their learning— at any age level, across content areas.

What questions are unanswered for you as an educator taking action for society? What are your biggest hopes and dreams for education and for our planet?

I would love to see an emphasis on creativity in the classroom, with a cross-curricular bent. I taught elementary school in a magnet school for environmental stewardship and loved having an integrated curriculum where writing and storytelling were present throughout the school day. I truly hope that students and teachers find ways to leverage the power of digital tools for storytelling to strengthen their communication and critical thinking skills.

If you have not yet connected with Monica, I encourage you to reach out to her and follow her educational shares on Twitter and Instagram. She tirelessly champions and advocates for today's educator and is a source of information and inspiration in my life.

CONSIDERING THE NARRATIVE: DIGITAL STORYTELLING

Digital literacies, as defined by the International Literacy Association's Literacy Glossary, are the literacies that "encompass the socially mediated ways of generating and interpreting online content through multiple modes (e.g., still and moving images, sounds, gestures, performances). Being digitally literate requires readers and writers to examine how the texts they consume, produce, and distribute online advocate for certain views while silencing other ideas" (2018).

Ability to Choose: Multi-Modal Options for Engagement

As students prepare their stories—content in the form of narratives, campaigns, creative writing pieces, position papers, scripts—it is imperative that we as teachers provide tools and systems that preserve voice and prioritize creativity in the expression of ideas. Technology as part of digital literacies can provide a library of options for offering choice. Multi-modal creations combine various modes of communication (audio, visual, tactile) and forms of media, including print, drawings, photography, audio, video, voice, and text. After in-depth study of each of the different modes and media, students can be offered options as they prepare to create their digital stories.

Text

Students can publish ideas, authored content, or stories digitally in the form of a blog or a webpage. **Adobe Spark** (spark.adobe.com) and **Weebly for Education** (education.weebly.com) offer free single-page websites for students. Text can be supported with images, videos, or weblinks.

4.2 The sixth-grade team behind #FoodMilesMatter created a website of tutorials at bit.ly/foodmilesmatter.

Nate makes Salad Skewers

Camila makes pesto from student harvested basil

Hayden explains tank maintainance

Video

With online spaces such as YouTube and livestreaming platforms such as Instagram, Twitter, Facebook, students today are savvy when it comes to creating videos. Favorite tools include **Adobe Spark Videos** (spark.adobe.com), **iMovie** (apple.com/imovie), **Flipgrid** (flipgrid.com), **Edpuzzle** (edpuzzle.com), and **WeVideo** (wevideo.com/education).

4.3 This elementary student video was created using Adobe Spark in El Centro, California.

ANDREW AREVALO (@GAMEBOYDREW)

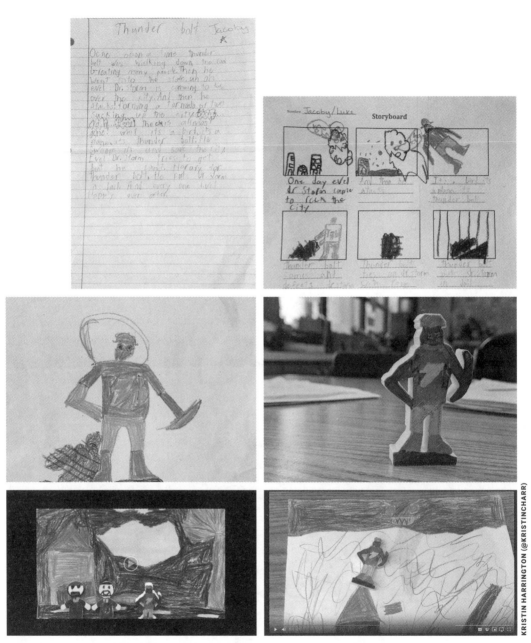

4.4 Elementary student used these steps to create stop-motion videos in Flagler County, Florida.

KRISTIN HARRINGTON (@KRISTINCHARR)

Digital Art

Digital art and graphics can be used to express ideas and stories visually and bring them to life. Students can draw, sketch, illustrate, and create slides with **Adobe Spark** (spark.adobe.com), **Canva** (canva.com), or **Microsoft PowerPoint** (office.microsoft.com/PowerPoint).

4.5 Elementary students in El Centro, California, created digital art on climate change using Adobe Spark.

4.6 A high school student in Fort Worth, Texas, used Adobe Spark to create a book cover for Colson Whitehead's novel *The Underground Railroad.*

4.7 Fourth-grade students in Shenzhen, China, created bilingual posters using Canva.

4.8 These black-out poems were created by fourth-grade students in Shenzhen, China, using Canva.

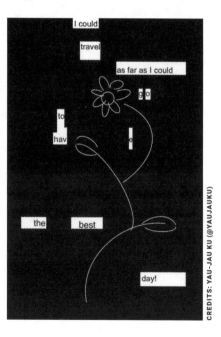

CREDITS: YAU-JAU KU (@YAUJAUKU)

Photography

Views of the world can be captured with cameras on mobile devices and enhanced with photo editing tools. As with all lessons, digital citizenship skills should be discussed and developed. For example, when incorporating photography, students should always get permission, even from friends, before posting pictures for a global audience.

4.9 Student Marigold Mioc (age 9, Alberta, Canada) shared this photo, Garbage to Greenhouse, in response to "Document Your Place on the Planet: Remember Earth," inspired by the Global Oneness Project film *Earthrise* in partnership with HundrED's Youth Ambassador Program (bit.ly/rememberearth).

Augmented Reality (AR) Stories

Students can use augmented reality (AR) to bring their stories to life by adding characters, motion, and sound to photos or videos. Check out the **JFK Moonshot app** (jfkmoonshot.org) to recreate and track the Apollo 11 mission or use the **3DBear app** (bit.ly/2MOcwiy) to create digital 3D AR stories through problem-based learning and creative storytelling.

4.10 The JFK Moonshot app is used to create AR stories at Moore Magnet Elementary in Winston-Salem, North Carolina.

CREDITS: PRINCIPAL SEAN GAILLARD (@SMGAILLARD)

Coding Stories

Students can use coding tools to create stories with characters and scenes, building in motion, storylines, plot twists, and more. Programs like **Scratch** (scratch.mit.edu), **ScratchJr** (scratchjr.org), and **Bloxels** (edu.bloxelsbuilder.com) can help students use coding, design, and their imaginations to solve real-world problems or express themselves creatively.

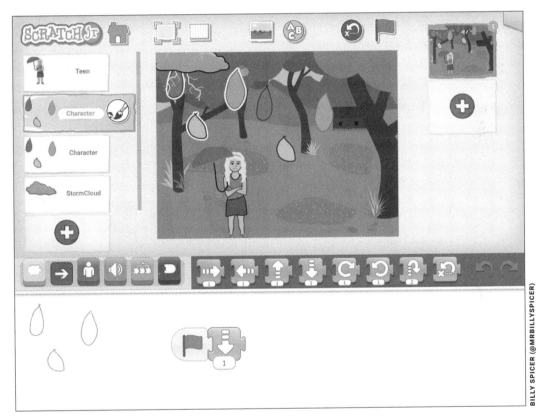

4.11 ScratchJr can be used to tell stories, as in this first-grade student's coding story from Chicago, Illinois.

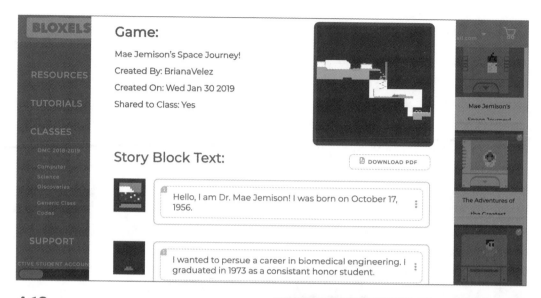

4.12 Students in Clermont, Florida, were assigned to research a famous African-American person and retell her or his life as a video game. This digital story was created using Bloxels.

RELIABLE AND RESPONSIBLE

Digital storytelling activities give students a chance to practice and develop digital citizenship skills through real-world experience. Consider using social good projects as an opportunity to discuss source reliability and bias. Think together on messages that are being shared, so that students can move from being responsible consumers to becoming responsible creators and providers of information. Explore options to better understand your audience as well.

Discuss ways to research and vet recipients of messages and seek out diverse perspectives for feedback. Talk about how your messages could go to audiences that you may not be able to anticipate or control, and run through scenarios as a group.

Post the following points in a visible place in the classroom as a reminder to students as they work:

- I use reliable sources.

- I am a responsible consumer.

- I am a responsible provider of information.

- I am a responsible creator of information.

- I seek out reliable audiences with diverse perspectives.

Edtech Resources for Diversity and Diverse Populations

As you consider the stories and perspectives of your students and yourself, there are several organizations that offer research and high-quality resources on diversity and creating culturally responsive classrooms. Though the process requires a great deal of thought and intentionality, here are a few leaders in the space that can help you get started:

- **ASIA SOCIETY CENTER FOR GLOBAL EDUCATION:** Diversity and culturally responsive classroom resources (asiasociety.org/education/diversity)

- **GLSEN:** LGBT-inclusive curriculum (glsen.org)

- **TEACHING TOLERANCE:** Classroom resources and professional development (tolerance.org)

- **WE NEED DIVERSE BOOKS:** Resources and book lists (diversebooks.org)

Using Edtech to Communicate across Lines of Difference

As we incorporate topics such as digital storytelling, global collaboration, and social good into instruction, edtech can help capture human experience and create safe spaces for dialogue and communication across lines of difference. We need to recognize and take conscious action on our own biases that we each bring to classrooms and to life. For me, learning through listening and shared experience has been a good start, but I will always need to do more through conscious action. Juli-Anne Benjamin, Brooklyn educator, school administrator, and board member of the International Literacy Association (ILA), is a trusted friend of mine who is always willing to help me do better in the work. Below are some recent thoughts she offered to me as I prepared this chapter.

Hi Juli-Anne! Please share a bit about your journey in your role as "educator as change agent."

My work as a teacher in primarily poor, marginalized, and underserved urban communities, spanning from the late 1990s to present, is sustainable only because change is the agent that is necessary for all pure transformation. I am an English educator and taught English language arts and literature for fourteen years before transitioning into administrative leadership, first as an instructional coach and now as vice principal. Throughout my career, change has always been consistent and a reliable source of professional success. I occupy revolutionary spaces in working to ensure that children have access to books, texts, and equitable tech in extremely poor environments.

Can you share all the places you've lived and worked, and one word or message that represents what each location means to you now?

As aforementioned, I primarily work in communities that suffer generational poverty and societal ills that affect people, such as joblessness, low literacy rates, drug addiction, and mental unwellness to name a few. As a new teacher, I encountered teenage moms (who had children while in school), thirty-five-year-old grandmothers attending parent-teacher conferences, and widespread family and community food insecurity daily. For decades, this was primarily in Bedford-Stuyvesant, Brooklyn, but it was no different in Pretoria, South Africa, or New Delhi, India, where I've lived and worked for years.

All three geographical locations differ vastly. Education and students also differ in demographic make-up and resources available, but all locations, especially within the work of educating children, are exemplified by one word and one effort: light.

You often talk about the importance of equity and access and quality learning for all our students. As someone doing the work, can you share on the related terms/ practices in education (e.g., social justice, culturally responsive teaching)? Which ones are we missing in education, if we want to go beyond the buzz and jargon and take steps of positive change?

Glad you asked this question. Indeed the buzz is around culturally responsive teaching (CRT), culturally responsive education (CRE), culturally responsive literacy instruction (CRLI) and culturally responsive pedagogy (CRP), and the mostly unused and misunderstood culturally sustaining pedagogy (CSP) (Paris & Alim, 2017).

The denotations of these acronyms—often tweeted, sourced, posted, designed into chats on social media—are largely referred to incorrectly when working with children in a granular framework of what is responsive to them and their needs—culturally, linguistically, and geographically. All of these terms build on and off the tradition- ally held and regularly practiced unresponsive practices of the non-black educator/ teacher and dominant culture being central to the way "all children learn." CRT "responds" to the student in front of you and is more than a white teacher playing hip-hop in the classroom to be "relatable" (although music and hip-hop are essential to any community of students that listen to and love that genre of music). Responding to one's culture must be curated through the relationship between teacher and child—between each other and in relationship to the work.

CSP is the change agent within all pedagogical frameworks that lives to build longev- ity and endurance in the race of cultural relevance across all ways that culture can be celebrated and eventually understood which will benefit children that are to be served.

Teachers are responsible for opening spaces and exposing children to all facets of global good in our world. They can create sustainable pathways to implementing change over time, thus turning the dial. We can position students as the leaders and the owners of our world as well as becoming active practitioners in the care of each other and our planet.

You can connect with Juli-Anne on Twitter at @JuliB224.

TAKE ACTION
CHECKING IN

How is your reading journey going? Use this Take ACTION point as a check-in to pause and consider your thinking at this time. Create a digital artifact (digital image, video, AR story, coding story, etc.) to capture your thinking on using ed-tech for social good at this moment. Share it on social media using the hashtag #TeachBoldly, or share it with students or colleagues at your school.

BOLD INVITATION
PUBLISH STUDENT WORK FOR GLOBAL AUDIENCES

One of my favorite lessons happened organically with one of the university courses I teach. In my elementary education course, Language Arts in the Elementary Years, I had students work collaboratively on a Google Doc to create a list of journal prompts by grade. Afterward, one student mentioned that she was excited to start teaching the following year so that she could use the prompts. That night, feeling happy that my students were excited, I shared a tweet on Twitter to see if any educators wanted to offer feedback on the prompts. By morning, I had five elementary teachers from all around the world messaging me, asking to join in. During our next class, my university students and I shared our Google Doc link with the teachers.

About a week later, we began to receive responses—not only from the teachers but also from their students. The teachers had each shared a prompt or two with their students, and they forwarded us many, many student papers. My students now had an authentic audience, as well as an authentic experience testing out their "teaching skills" because they were able to review and respond to the student journal entries. It was extraordinary.

Consider finding ways to work with your students to publish their stories for a global audience. Take bold action on providing opportunities for feedback and revision based on the perspectives of others.

MY PEACEMAKER PROFILE ACTIVITY #4
REQUESTING FEEDBACK

Now that you have started developing your PeaceMAKER Profile, consider requesting feedback from a peer. Your peer can be someone in your school, someone from your PLN, or an administrator or trusted mentor. As you prepare to share your profile, consider these questions:

- Who to ask?

- How to ask?

- How to record feedback?

- How to develop and grow from feedback?

- How to offer appreciation for review and feedback?

After requesting and receiving feedback on your plan, think about how to incorporate new ideas or new ways of approaching ideas. Are there other peer reviewers who could offer a different view than yours to help improve your work? How might you approach them? What are your next steps?

You can also use this template to record your experience:

My PeaceMAKER Profile

Request Feedback

PLANNING

1. Who to ask?

2. How to ask?

3. How to record feedback?

4. How to develop and grow from feedback?

5. How to offer appreciation for review and feedback?

RECEIVED FEEDBACK

NEW IDEAS BASED ON FEEDBACK

Purposeful Actions for the Good of All

Estella Owoimaha-Church, High School Teacher, Global Teacher Prize Finalist, California, USA
Twitter: @eochurch

My friend Estella Owoimaha-Church is a social good hero. She is an English and theater teacher, Global Teacher Prize finalist, TeachSDGs Ambassador, Rock Your World Ambassador, human rights and education activist, and world-changer. She encourages her California high school students to "take a stand where you can." Through a yearly social action project called Arts in Service, students select matters of personal significance, then work in groups of three or four to design and craft an action that utilizes their skills as artists.

They work through the lens of either the Universal Declaration of Human Rights or the Sustainable Development Goals (SDGs) (see chapter 1), and throughout the process, they discover their own potential to create real change in the world. Here are four student stories, told by Estella:

> The first year we completed this Art in Service project, one student was committed to improving representation for women of color in media. She hosted and directed her own show that semester, featuring plays and monologues that highlight women of various ethnicities and religions around the world. She raised money at both shows and was able to coordinate collaboration among students from several clubs and organizations on our campus. The money she raised went to support the peer mentor program of Media Done Responsibly, a local nonprofit working to improve media representation of all people.

That same year, a young man with autism spectrum disorder (ASD) committed himself to supporting other students with ASD. Knowing social cues were an area in which he and the others needed improvement, he planned weekend outings and movie dates with his pals. He worked hard as a mentor to help them get their homework and projects in on time. He supported them as technicians in the program; he even helped them compete at a regional festival for the first time. When he felt successful here, he began advocating for others with ASD outside of our school and with larger organizations in Los Angeles. To this day, he returns to help support other students—whether they have ASD or not.

Last year, a couple of students created a social media campaign they called WomIn Power. Their plan was to highlight all the women in their everyday lives they viewed as super-human—mostly teachers. They wanted to highlight the power of women across ethnic, generational, and religious divides. They created a beautiful scrapbook featuring photos and personal narratives of women in the community, and then created digital versions to be shared on Twitter.

And that's just my theater students. Last year, I began implementing Innovation and Climate Action Projects in my English course. The service project ideas that have come out of them have been just as amazing. One of my favorites was a group of young men who happen to be below a fifth-grade reading level. Their academic self-concepts and overall confidence were pretty low. They wanted to deal with SDG4: Quality Education. After a month of debate and deliberation, they settled on "Thinking Homies." Their goal was to support students who were often underserved on our campus. They felt like only AP and honors students were geared towards college and received the extra support from teachers, so they wanted to create an after-school tutoring service for students who were like them. The young men also wanted to host a weekly check-in the form of a circle to remain confidential. They figured this would not only help improve the confidence level of kids and improve grades, but also mitigate trauma, bad behavior, or violence.

Each year, Estella's students use their voices and creativity to use edtech for good. Taking action on racial profiling, body image, lack of LGBTQ visibility, bullying, misogyny, identity development, and global sustainability issues, these young adults are working to make a difference—a difference created by them, on issues that matter to them personally.

Estella also shared her thoughts on our responsibility as educators to take bold action against systems of oppression in our schools and communities. Here are three actions she encounters in her work each day that she believes we all need to take on as teachers:

1. Speak up when a peer says something racist or homophobic.

2. Offer to lead in-service or professional development on topics that may be controversial or in need of discussion based on circumstances.

3. Correct a person or other teacher if she or he misgenders a transgender student.

5

CONSCIOUS CONSUMERS: ADDING CONTEXT TO THE TOOL

Educators today are playing an active role in the selection and creation of curriculum and educational tools. This chapter considers how educators can collaborate with edtech companies to improve products and impact student learning.

Helping Hands by Max Yang, Grade 8
Medium: Marker
Donna Guerin, Classroom Teacher
Renaissance Secondary School, Denver, CO, USA

INSPIRATION: Making Their Mark

We gathered at the corner of East Ninety-Second Street and Lexington Avenue in New York City for the Social Good Summit, organized by the United Nations Foundation and Mashable. Seated in the beautiful yet modest 92Y cultural community center, we took our seats for a day of action and change.

Taking the stage were prime ministers and activists, writers and actors, presidents of companies and presidents of countries. There were also students and young changemakers who were sharing ways technology, new media, and education were intersecting and redefining our understanding of human progress.

I was one of a small number of educators in attendance, and I was determined to learn how we as teachers could support students as they unlock technology's potential to make the world a better place. Listening to conversations on technologies such as blockchain, artificial intelligence, and machine learning, I could see that the future for which we are preparing our students is filled with hope, progress, and rapidly changing technologies that are triggering new products and new ways of working.

That day made it clear that we are moving into a future that advances as soon as we learn it, and I saw the need for me as an educator to be adaptable and prepared to pivot in unanticipated ways. Two stories stuck with me and kept me thinking about the types of jobs my students will encounter in the future.

5.1 New Story Charity co-founder Alexandria Lafci shares on 3D printed homes at the Social Good Summit 2018.

New Story Charity

Society today faces a global homelessness crisis and extreme poverty, but young innovators like Alexandria Lafci are racing to build new solutions

that will allow for more equitable opportunities for all. For Alexandria and
her organization New Story Charity
(newstorycharity.org), housing is a
human right. "It's irresponsible not to
try," she says. With the support of other
organizations and companies that are
also ready to take action on big ideas,
such as ICON Construction Technologies,
she and her team have developed 3D
printed homes that can be built for
$4,000 in as little as twelve hours. At
the time of the Social Good Summit, the
impact of their invention was already
taking shape, and they described an entire community of safe, storm-resistant
3D-printed homes in El Salvador they had
completed. With ingenuity in design com-
bined with a belief in a better world and
future, this is just the beginning for them.

5.2 3D-printed homes can be made for $4,000 in under one day.

5.3 3D-printed home communities are being used to help end homelessness in El Salvador, Mexico, Haiti, and Bolivia.

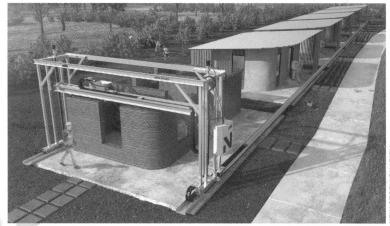

NEW STORY CHARITY

5.4 3D-printed homes allow technology to support humanity.

Mobile Phones for Girls

That day at the Social Good Summit, we learned that technology and innovations in social good can also support the human right of gender equality. Zuriel Oduwole, a sixteen-year-old filmmaker and education advocate, shared her mission to break barriers internationally with access to technology for all. She cited landmark research that included interviews with 3,000 boys and girls from twenty-five countries about the use and impact of mobile technologies (Vodafone, 2018). The findings demonstrated that because boys are one and a half times more likely to own a phone, girls are being left behind and have to negotiate for access.

Often shamed for being seen with a phone, girls in many parts of the world are unable to access the technologies they need for their learning, safety, and well-being. Zuriel, after sharing that she has met with twenty-eight presidents and prime ministers and 26,000 students worldwide on the importance of education for girls, announced how the nonprofit organization Girl Effect (girleffect.org) and the Vodafone Foundation (vodafone.com/content/foundation.html) were connecting to drive change by providing mobile phones and service to more than seven million girls in Africa and Asia within five years. According to Zuriel, this will enable more girls to experience how technology can empower them to ask questions, get advice, and share their journeys with the world—just as it had for her.

5.5 Sixteen-year-old filmmaker and education advocate Zuriel Oduwole shares on gender equality and mobile phones at the Social Good Summit 2018.

5.6 Girl Effect and Vodafone are providing seven million girls in Africa and Asia with mobile phones and service to support gender equality.

EDUCATORS AS INSTRUCTIONAL DESIGNERS

Innovation is the driver of social action and global change. Just as organizations like New Story and Girl Effect are challenging norms in industry, technologies are changing the ways classrooms operate in areas of teaching, learning, thinking, and communicating.

Edtech companies and organizations progress by building on established learning theory as they devise technologies and innovations. As companies develop edtech products, educators must be part of the conversation to ensure students are kept at the center of design decisions. We need teaching and learning to be grounded in research with clear evidence of impact and building of skills.

Unlike years ago, when classroom teachers were handed boxed curricula to follow lockstep in a linear process of instruction, today's educator can play an active role in designing, creating, and choosing edtech tools that support dynamic teaching and learning.

HELPING EDTECH COMPANIES DEFINE AND SHAPE THEIR PRODUCTS

Edtech companies need teachers and students. And, because we are teachers who understand that repetition is a strategy for memory and learning, I will repeat that: *Edtech companies need teachers and students.*

For edtech companies to create products that can positively impact learning and increase productivity and efficiency of transferring knowledge, it is essential they understand how their products are used. Surprisingly, though, there are few structures in place to support communication between classrooms and companies. I've found that many edtech companies say, "We don't want to bother teachers. We know they are busy." And many teachers don't know that the opportunity to build a relationship with an edtech company is desired or even possible. To keep the design of instructional products moving in the right direction, it is imperative that we find ways to talk and work together. Before we get to how we might do that, let's get into some terminology to help create a shared language.

Cut out the Jargon

Although edtech companies and educators are heading in a similar direction with a similar goal, they often use different language from one another. As edtech companies work to better understand teacher-speak and the acronyms of education, here are a few key terms used in the start-up world of innovation to help educators learn the language of edtech.

Accelerator Programs

Accelerator programs are used to help individuals with ideas or programming expertise move their ideas from concept to market. Accelerators typically provide resources, mentoring, and seed funding to start-up companies in exchange for shares or percentage of ownership. Many edtech products that teachers and students use today originated in accelerator programs. Examples include **Imagine K12** (part of Y combinator; imaginek12.com), **xEdu** (xedu.co), and **StartEd** (started.com).

Bootstrapped

As an alternative to launching an edtech company with the support and funding of an incubator or accelerator program, edtech entrepreneurs may choose to self-fund their start-up initiatives. Originating from the phrase "pull yourself up by your own bootstraps," bootstrapped companies have autonomy in decision-making and funding as they develop.

Beta Test

In software development, beta testing is the product phase where members of an intended user group test out early versions of a product. This typically occurs prior to the full launch or release of a product or feature.

Freemium

A freemium business model offers options for product use, so that users can choose between a free-of-charge basic level and fee-based premium levels. Premium levels typically provide more advanced features or enhanced levels of support.

Unicorn

A unicorn company is a privately held technology start-up company valued at more than one billion dollars. The term "unicorn" denotes the near-mythical nature of companies that have achieved this level of success (Lee, 2013).

User Feedback and User Experience

Most edtech companies aim to incorporate user feedback into product design and development at every stage. A User Experience (UX) designer is responsible for prototyping, researching, testing, and reporting on the ongoing quality of experience for users.

GOOD FOR CLASSROOMS AND GOOD FOR THE WORLD

As instructional decision-makers and content curators, it is critical that educators have a firm understanding of a company or organization's intention for development. What is their *why*? Do their hopes and dreams for education and for the world align with yours as an educator? Do they position and prioritize people and pedagogy ahead of the tool?

With choice comes responsibility. As the gatekeepers to the classroom and to instruction, you and your students must critically examine and evaluate not only new digital resources but also the core values of the companies and organizations building those resources. Following are several business structure models that tend to be good for classrooms and good for the world.

Nonprofit Organizations

Nonprofit organizations are organized as private foundations or public charities with a mission to further a particular social cause or to offer a human service. Nonprofits are accountable to program recipients, volunteers, donors, and the public, and they offer transparency to all stakeholders. Because they are mission-driven, nonprofit organizations aim to create a positive impact in a community. They depend on sound research to help them improve their offerings and to advance public policy and public awareness.

Education nonprofits account for more than 17% of all nonprofit organizations, and types include education member and service organizations, education product developers, and education content creators (National Council of Nonprofits, 2018; councilofnonprofits.org). Examples include DonorsChoose, Sesame Street Workshop, the Collaborative for Academic, Social, and Emotional Learning (CASEL), and ISTE.

Non-governmental Organizations (NGOs)

Non-governmental organizations (NGOs) are nonprofit organizations independent of government bodies. They are founded by groups of citizens with a shared commitment to a humanitarian, educational, environmental, or human rights issue. Members of an NGO can operate at local, national, or international levels. NGOs in education work to offer solutions through service, policy advancement, and advocacy with an international footprint. Examples of education NGOs include the International Association of University Presidents and Art Education for the Blind.

B Corporations

A B Corporation (or B Corp) is a type of for-profit corporation that is purpose-driven and committed to addressing social and environmental issues through responsible and mindful business practices. B Corps commit to creating value for local and global communities, employees, and the environment by balancing purpose and profit, and their performance is certified by the nonprofit B Lab. B Lab's "B Corp Declaration of Interdependence" states:

As B Corporations and leaders of this emerging economy, we believe:

- *That we must be the change we seek in the world.*

- *That all business ought to be conducted as if people and place mattered.*

- *That, through their products, practices, and profits, businesses should aspire to do no harm and benefit all.*

- *To do so requires that we act with the understanding that we are each dependent upon another and thus responsible for each other and future generations. (B Lab, 2018)*

Patagonia, Ben & Jerry's, The Honest Company, and Klean Kanteen are widely known B Corps. Examples of B Corps in education include AltSchool, Participate, Kickstarter, and Hootsuite.

OPEN EDUCATIONAL RESOURCES

In addition to products created by companies or organizations, teachers can access open educational resources. Open educational resources (OERs) are teaching and learning materials that are free and available online for use by all. As referenced and recommended in the Office of Educational Technology's National Technology Plan (US DOE, 2017; tech.ed.gov/files/2017/01/NETP17.pdf), OERs can range from full online courses or digital textbooks to images, videos, or assessment items. Gaining in familiarity and use by educators over the past several years, OERs offer an equitable alternative to textbooks and pre-packaged curricula, enabling classroom teachers to curate and customize resources based on need and by purpose.

Andrew Marcinek, former chief open education advisor for the US Department of Education (Twitter: @andycinek), was the first lead for #GoOpen, a movement to help PK—12 school districts replace costly textbooks with educational materials that are shareable and modifiable. "#GoOpen places creative content control back into the hands of the educator," Andrew shared. "#GoOpen seeks to reinvest in the teaching profession by repurposing money used for overpriced, out-of-date textbooks and investing it in teacher training and development."

By using OERs and committing to #GoOpen, districts, schools, and teachers can provide all students, regardless of location on the planet, with an equitable, relevant educational experience. What's up next for OERs and #GoOpen? Andrew offered his vision for the future: "I hope that by 2025 schools are no longer purchasing textbooks, and they are relying upon and compensating educators for their work in designing and implementing educational materials that are shareable, modifiable, accessible, and relevant for all students."

EVALUATION AND USE OF SOFTWARE AND HARDWARE

Educators and educational leaders are increasingly aware of initiative-fatigue and the "one-more-new-thing-to-do" trend we are seeing in schools and classrooms today. With marketing of edtech software and hardware aimed directly at teachers and students, the space is becoming a noisy one. Educators need to actively and boldly engage in the process of selection and adoption, and position themselves as savvy, critical consumers of products and tools.

Recognizing the need to see past cute characters and snazzy graphics, educators are demanding high-quality and research-based products for their students. We in our profession are uniquely positioned to test out new tools and programs in our classrooms, but we need to be judicious and intentional in our commitments to sustained and thoughtful use over time.

Selection Criteria for Tools and Programs

The job description of a classroom teacher is evolving to include the roles of instructional designer and content creator. As we have examined previously, teachers are no longer passive in the process of tool selection and program adoption. Educational leaders are including teachers in decision-making processes and are often relying on teachers to provide guidance based on data and anticipated need.

If you have not yet been a part of these types of conversations, here is how you can prepare and arm yourself with the necessary information and analytics to get and keep the resources you need for your students.

TABLE 5.1 Examples of Selection Criteria for Edtech Tools and Programs

Area of Selection Criteria	"Looks Fors"	"Watch Out Fors"
Mission-driven organization	Mission is clearly identified and centered on student learning	Mission is neither directly related to education nor focused on student learning
Student privacy	Stated student privacy policy Evidence of COPPA and FERPA compliance Evidence of EU-US Privacy Shield Framework compliance	Minimal evidence of commitment to student privacy or online safeguards
Research-based content	Content is aligned to standards and best practices in K–12 education Clear horizontal and vertical trajectories to scaffold and personalize learning Alignment to ISTE Standards	Content is random and lacks clarity in design Little to no evidence of basis of research or alignment to standards of practice
Provides reporting	Ability to record, track, and report on student learning over time	No ability to monitor and report on progress
Contributes to the body of research in education and edtech	White papers Case studies Participation in qualitative/quantitative research studies	No evidence of conducting or participating in research

Area of Selection Criteria	"Looks Fors"	"Watch Out Fors"
Values teacher and student feedback	Seeks out and reports on teacher/student feedback Product informed by feedback Engages with teachers on social media Teacher ambassador programs	Feedback and teacher-centric engagements not evident
Supports sustained use	Mobile friendly Integrations with LMS Pathways to sustained use over time detailed Certifications and partnerships	Designed for single-instance use Lacks ability to effectively integrate into current instructional practices
Commitment to equity and access	Clear commitment to equity, access, and personalized learning	Bias is present Equity and access are not clearly addressed
Focus on creation	Ability for students to create, collaborate, curate, and express ideas and understandings Student agency and choice Emphasis on student engagement	Focus on student consumption of information Students not able to have choice or options Emphasis on compliance
Opportunity for students to take action	Opportunity for students to take action on passions or beliefs Opportunity for students to share perspectives and get feedback on ideas Opportunity to connect at local and global levels	Content is static and lacks ability for students to act and/or interact
Commitment to sustainability and social good	Commitment to giving and social good	No clear commitment to giving or social good
Professional development (PD) opportunities for educators	Teachers are supported with PD Webinars, videos, blog posts, Twitter chats, onsite trainings	Professional development is not addressed

TAKE ACTION
CONNECT THROUGH SOCIAL NETWORKS

Conversations around edtech and instructional design are alive on Twitter 24/7. Connect asynchronously by following edtech organizations on social media and tagging them on posts and tweets. Be sure to follow their hashtag and watch for any Twitter chats they may join.

You can also connect in synchronous Twitter chats. Join the Twitter chat #edtechbridge, which invites educators and edtech companies to come together each month in online conversations. You can message educator and chat moderator Steve Isaacs at @mr_isaacs for more information.

BOLD INVITATION
BE THE CONTEXT

Remember the statement at the start of the chapter: *Edtech companies need teachers and students.* We can teach boldly by providing useful context for edtech companies. I invite you to connect with an edtech company/organization. As you organize your outreach plan, here are a few tips to help get you connected:

- Consider blogging about your experience using the tool or product and share the link with the edtech company through email or on Twitter.

- Research to find the contact information for the customer representative who covers your geographic area and send them an email.

- Visit the booths of the edtech company at conferences and introduce yourself as a customer.

- Check to see if the company has an educator ambassador group and research the application process.

- Document your process and share with your instructional team or school leader.

MY PEACEMAKER PROFILE ACTIVITY #5
RESOURCE REVIEW

Ready to take action on your big ideas and instructional goals with edtech? For your your fifth activity in building your PeaceMAKER Profile, select and analyze an edtech tool or product you intend to use with your class.

STEP 1: Select a tool or program to review. Determine your "Look Fors" and take a "website walk" in which you tour and carefully review the edtech company's website. Use the Examples of Selection Criteria for Edtech Tools and Programs in Table 5.1 as a starting point with the Activity Sheet in Table 5.2 (printable version available at jenwilliamsedu.com/peacemaker-profile.html). Be sure to keep in mind your own school's mission, initiatives, and strategic plan.

STEP 2: When you feel confident in the integrity and soundness of the product, tool, or program, you are now ready to determine if it is the right fit for your instructional design and student learning objectives. Does the tool align with your curricular plans? Does it allow for the extension of ideas and expression of thought? Will students see the logical connections between content and use, or will it cause confusion and distract from skill building and learning outcomes?

STEP 3: Arm yourself with knowledge. Before diving in with your students, be sure to access any offered professional development resources. Test out the tool or application in your classroom using your school devices and Wi-Fi connection.

STEP 4: Dedicate time and thought to determining the best way to introduce students to the tool or program. Here are some practical ideas for implementation:

- Be explicit and tell students your goal in incorporating the new form of technology into teaching and learning.

- Clearly state expectations for appropriate use and explore possible solutions to any anticipated challenges.

- Offer opportunities for continued use over time. Provide time for exploration and encourage curiosity and creative thinking. Hope for students to find new uses that you did not expect or plan for.

STEP 5: Document, document, document.

- Record student testimonials.

- Record observations as field notes.

- Record formative and summative assessment data.

STEP 6: Gather your results and plan for the future. Share your findings with your instructional team and school leaders. If you have determined that the technology enriches teaching and learning in your classroom, establish a plan for sustained use.

ENGAGING STUDENTS IN THE PROCESS: In education, we ourselves must engage in thoughtful exercises of digital literacy and digital citizenship as we aim to provide students with choice, agency, and skills of discernment and critical thinking. Students too can be part of the process of selecting the right tools and products for the classroom. It is our job as teachers to get them involved and engaged. Introduce students to the fundamental concepts and purposes of technologies and help them build an understanding of their role as consumers. Explicitly cover the steps and actions of research, selection, and evaluation, and discuss how to ensure tools are (1) reliable, (2) relevant, and (3) responsible sources of information.

TABLE 5.2 My PeaceMAKER Profile Activity #5

Reliable, Relevant, and Responsible Resources	
Edtech Resource Report	
Name of Tool/Product:	
Reviewer:	Date:
Website:	Social Media:
Organizational Mission:	
Funding Source/Business Model:	
Commitment to Student Privacy:	
Purpose of Tool:	
Alignment to Standards/Research:	
Targeted Competencies/Skills:	
Reporting Methods:	
Evidence of Thought Leadership (White papers, case studies, research studies):	
Commitment to Obtaining Teacher/Student Feedback:	
Commitment to Sustained Use, Equity, and Access:	
Opportunity for Student Creation, Agency, and Choice:	
Ability for Students to Take Action on Ideas:	
Professional Development Opportunities for Educators:	
Recommendations Based on Review:	

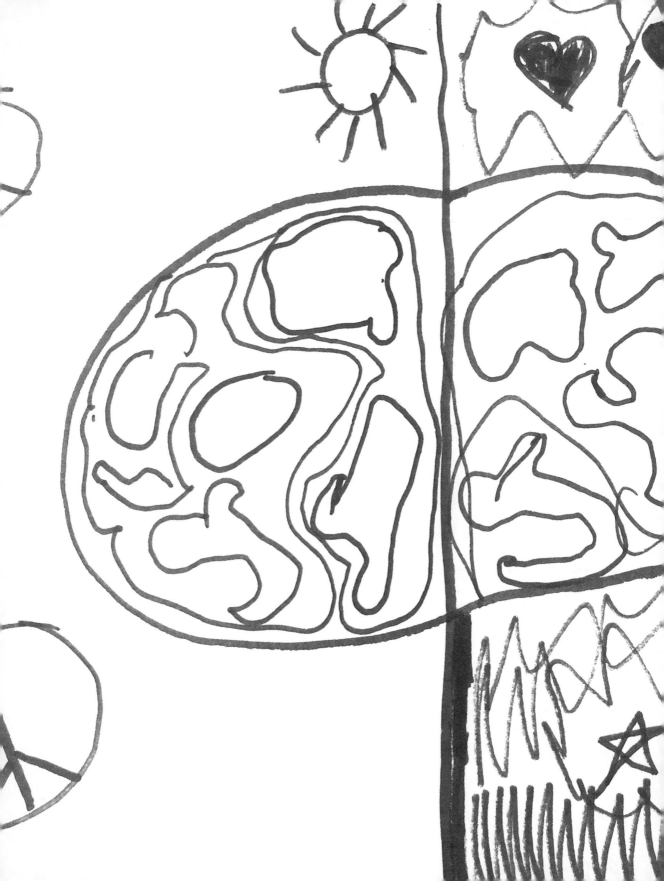

6

I'D LIKE TO TEACH THE WORLD TO

_____.

This concluding chapter focuses on the professional learning of the reader and on what you as the reader would like to learn and then share with the world. As the architect of your own learning experience, you will be able to complete the phrase, "I'd like to teach the world to _____ ," and make a plan to reach that goal.

Untitled drawing by Ellie Buis, Age 6
Medium: Marker
Belleair, Florida, USA
Artist note: *Everyday the sun will rise and fall and the moon will rise and fall on our world. And no matter what it will always happen.*

INSPIRATION: Pushing Beyond the Edge of Your Lane to Make a Difference

Professional learning is one of the most essential elements of our work as educators. But as I have learned from my friend Jacob Sule (@SuleJacobS) in Nigeria, the value of learning is not always determined by the affordances one is offered. A brilliant young law student at Osun State University who aspires to shape policy for his country and for our world, Jacob is concerned not only for his own future but for that of his community and country. After seeing that students in rural communities were leaving school without the basic skills they needed to be employable, he assembled and mobilized other law students to volunteer with him in the schools and help develop a love of reading and learning among the young students there.

Trained as lawyers, not as educators, they recognized that they did not have the skills they needed, so in early 2018 they messaged me on Twitter and asked if I could help. We arranged to meet for an hour-long video call to make a plan. To make sure they would have reliable Wi-Fi, they traveled one hour by bus to an internet cafe. Dressed in their best clothes, they gathered around one laptop computer for our session, eager for new learning. I could see that they were hanging on every word I said. For them, learning was lifewide. It wasn't just in their one lane with a single trajectory. It was everywhere.

In the months that followed, Jacob and his young adult volunteers (ages seventeen to twenty-three) continued to work with me. They accessed and reviewed the latest research on literacy and literacy practice online, they took their new NGO **iRead to Live Initiative** (ireadtolive.org) to the Ministry of Education in Nigeria, and they organized Nigeria's first Edcamp, **Edcamp Nigeria** (edcampnigeria.weebly.com), with special help and guidance from Hadley Ferguson, co-founder and executive director of **Edcamp Foundation** (edcamp.org).

Now a volunteer group of thirty-five Nigerian law students, they travel to schools each week to teach. They go into classrooms, take on half of a teacher's eighty students, and work with them on lessons—without books, paper, technology, or, in some cases, even tables.

6.1 Jacob Sule and several of his volunteers gather around a computer for our video session.

In fall 2018, Jacob was recognized by the International Literacy Association on its 30 Under 30 List as one of the most influential young literacy leaders of the world. With little money or resources, barely even Wi-Fi or a working computer, Jacob is making it happen—for his community and its future, and for our world and our future.

6.2 Jacob works with a group of students in Nigeria.

LIFEWIDE LEARNING

Many of today's high school graduates will live to be 100 years old (Christensen et al., 2009), compared to an average lifespan of only forty years 200 years ago. Today's high school graduates will have an average of twelve to fifteen jobs and will face disruptive innovations the entire time (US Bureau of Labor Statistics, 2019). As soon as they learn one job, along will come another with new skills they'll need to learn.

This understanding of the future requires us to rethink our conceptions of school and work. In our traditional view, school takes place during childhood; learning is the focus as the child develops skills and gains knowledge. Then there is a dramatic shift from school to work, and learning—the primary activity of the young person's life up to that point—is abruptly replaced with work. But what if we were to instead view both school and work as integral to every phase of life? How might it look if we had threads of learning woven throughout every one of our years? How might we prioritize not only lifelong learning but also lifewide learning?

IMPACTS OF A NEW WORKFORCE

Today's innovation invites young people joining the workforce to invent the future, and we are already starting to see major shifts in the way people work. Meetings can be less about boardrooms and more about virtual chat rooms. Women are showing that they can and should be allowed to balance work and life, as evidenced by Prime Minister Jacinda Ardern of New Zealand, who brought her three-month-old daughter into the United Nations General Assembly Hall meetings in 2018. (She is only the second elected world leader ever to give birth while in office.)

So, where does that leave us—in teaching and learning and in school and work? As we move into a future that will advance just as we learn it, we as teachers also need to be adaptable.

LEARNING FOR KNOWLEDGE AND FOR WELL-BEING

Educational inequities become even greater as people age. Globally, only 1% of adults older than forty are enrolled in formal education (OECD, 2018), even though jobs require new and continually updated skills. As we consider lifewide learning and its impact on well-being, we can look to countries such as Norway, Sweden, and Switzerland, which prioritize learning for all and at every age. Not surprisingly, studies have shown that these three countries also have the happiest aging populations (Helliwell, Layard, & Sachs, 2019).

But even in those areas, socio-economic status still influences equitable learning. It is common for people with advanced degrees to receive almost twice as much funding from their employers for continued learning and advancement. Learning becomes exponential, making it even harder for individuals without degrees to advance and keep up.

Considering all this, how do we as teachers move forward with our learning? How might we push beyond the edges of our lanes for lifewide experiences?

ANDRAGOGY: ADULT LEARNING THEORY

As we consider the professional learning of educators, it is important to note that adults and children learn in different ways. Educators with expertise in learning theory and experience in teaching may instinctively apply student learning principles to adult professional development (PD). But because we as adults think and learn differently from our students, principles of adult learning theory should be considered and applied instead.

PEDAGOGY: *"leading children"*

ANDRAGOGY: *"art and science of teaching adults"*

149

Adult learning theory, or andragogy, was developed by Malcolm Knowles and his colleagues in their work designing adult training programs (1970). A specialized instructional design and delivery method for adults, andragogy is a learner-centric approach that prioritizes engagement. Described by Knowles as "an emerging technology for adult learning," andragogy makes four assumptions about adult learning:

- Adults move from dependency to self-directedness;

- Adults draw upon their reservoirs of experience for learning;

- Adults seek learning when they assume new roles; and

- Adults want to solve problems and apply new knowledge immediately (Knowles, 1970).

BE THE ARCHITECT OF YOUR OWN LEARNING

Educators today are taking control of their own learning. They create customized plans of professional development that reflect their professional interests and that are responsive to the need for new or deepened understanding of the world. Rapid advancements in technology and innovation reinforce teachers' desires to learn as they see the need for new skills and new ways of instructing and communicating in the classroom.

Educators describe their ideal PD with words such as *inspirational, empowering, relevant, social, supercharged,* and *fun,* and to get to that type of experience, they are blending informal learning with structured, formal learning events. Recent trends in modern professional development are transforming the traditional processes of learning and are positioning teachers as the architects of their own professional journeys.

PD Trend #1: Backward Design Planning

Many educators look at the end goal that connects to a larger vision, then work backward to create PD plans. With a clearly defined, intentional purpose, educators can strategically match learning opportunities to goals and create steps to achieving knowledge on specific topics.

For instance, a globally minded educator seeking to create an international audience for student writing may want to better understand both standards of practice and tech tools for collaboration. This teacher might select an online conference for learning more on international writing standards, a book study on global collaboration with peers in a Professional Learning Network (PLN), and expert interviews with educational consultants from several ed-tech companies. With an intentional focus on gaining skills and competencies, this educator can effectively meet stated goals to support instruction and student learning.

PD Trend #2: Responsive Options

The one-size-fits-all model of PD is being reimagined with modern formats that respond to varying learning preferences. Educators looking for flexible options are finding that choices can be social and multimodal, incorporating text, audio, video, and graphics. These learner-centric offerings empower educators to take charge of professional growth in their search for creating connections between content, experience, and available resources.

Instead of mandated sit-and-listen PD designed for many, personalized learning experiences can connect educators to their core beliefs about teaching and learning. Options here include joining Twitter chats, reading blogs, listening to podcasts, participating in a social media learning challenge, joining a PD Flipgrid, or tuning in for webinars, TED Talks, or live social media sharing on Facebook Live, Instagram Stories, or Twitter Live.

The #whatisschool community is a good example of this. A virtual space with a hashtag, Twitter chat, and blog, #whatisschool invites educators from across the world to express ideas and opinions about schooling and the state of education through participation in hour-long Twitter discussions. Each week, educators join chat moderator Craig Kemp (@mrkempnz) as he and a weekly guest moderator guide an online dialogue with six questions. With new topics each week, participating educators have a voice in shaping the future of education by sharing their experiences, concerns, recommendations, interests, and hopes for the world. Join #whatisschool any week on Twitter. Chat times are listed on Craig's website (mrkempnz.com/category/whatisschool).

Other popular Twitter chats for educators looking to take action on social good include:

- **#globaledchat:** Global Edchat; Moderator: Heather Singmaster, @hsingmaster

- **#dtk12chat:** Design Thinking K—12 Chat; Co-Moderator: Dan Ryder, @WickedDecent

- **#edtechchat:** Edtech Chat; Co-Moderator: Susan Bearden, @s_bearden

- **Other hashtags related to social good in education:** #TeachBoldly, #edtech4good, #MicrosoftEdu, #EduColor, #TeachSDGs, and #ILAChat.

PD Trend #3: Micro-Credentialing and Digital Badging

In addition to being empowered to design personalized plans for global professional growth, educators are now charged with determining how learning will be demonstrated and validated for recognition. Evidencing practices, such as micro-credentialing and digital badging, can serve to document professional growth in ways that are interoperable and universally recognizable for educators around the world. These competency-based models provide systems that can recognize professional learning and the sharing of best practices regardless of time, place, or rate of learning.

Global educators seeking to document skills and competencies in PD plans in a practical and focused manner can earn micro-credentials through multiple organizations and agencies. Once an appropriate program is selected, an educator can follow these steps:

1. Select skills or competencies for development.

2. Collect and organize evidencing materials (e.g., class videos, photos capturing work, video logs of progress, field notes, etc.).

3. Submit evidence in the form of a portfolio or digital artifact to showcase development of target skills.

Following submission, field experts review the provided documentation to ensure established standards of mastery are met, then recognition is awarded. Often, digital badges are offered to serve as a recognizable validation of accomplishments, positioning educators as valued resources in their global learning networks. To learn more about micro-credentials and digital badging, be sure to follow #badgechat, #CollaborativePD, and @participate on Twitter.

PD Trend #4: Sustained Inquiry

For a true shift in practice, educators need to develop depth of knowledge over extended periods of time and across multiple learning environments. Sustained inquiry allows educators to approach questions through an iterative process of trial, evaluation, redefining, and reimagining. Learning can be collaborative, networked, and continuous. By working together in connected spaces (both within schools and within virtual PLNs), educators can collaborate with others and gain understanding from diverse perspectives and reflective thinking.

Viewed by many as the mainstay of connected learning and sustained inquiry, Twitter has evolved into a virtual space where educators can take ownership of their professional growth. After using Twitter as an entry point for dialogue and discussion, many educators extend their explorations and conversations with new colleagues to other networked platforms, such as blogging, Flipgrid, Voxer, Periscope, and Instagram.

Schools too are creating social media accounts, using school-specific hashtags to share information with their own communities of teachers, and also to tell the world about the great things happening in their classrooms. Examples of school-wide hashtags include:

- #MooreTogether, #TrendthePositive, #CelebrateMonday
  Moore Magnet Elementary School, Winston-Salem, North Carolina, USA
  Principal Sean Gaillard, @smgaillard

- #GatorRunRocks, #EveryoneMatters, #TheBestThingISawToday
  Gator Run Elementary, Weston, Florida, USA
  Principal Keith Peters, @principalkp

PD Trend #5: Crowd-Sourced Learning

Unlike traditional top-down approaches to PD, participatory learning opportunities garner the collective input of educators through crowdsourced, collaborative practices. By incorporating educator voice and enlisting all educators in the decision-making process, learning experiences put teachers at the center of their own learning.

Educators can dive deeply into relevant dialogue with peers and experts. These practices are revolutionizing professional learning, making the peer-to-peer learning movement the "PD of choice" for many educators. As part of this shift, models such as mastermind groups, think tanks, and Edcamps are becoming primary components of PD plans for many educators of the world.

Mastermind Groups

Mastermind groups have recently gained in popularity in education circles. Educators interested in exploring a topic with people outside of their current network can join or organize a mastermind group. Typically, mastermind groups have between six and ten people from different areas and backgrounds. For instance, you may be interested in exploring the topic of giving students an authentic global audience for their writing or digital creations. To examine this topic, you invite five other educators (e.g., an elementary teacher, a music teacher, a high school administrator, a professor at a community college, and a strategist from an edtech company—all people you have met either on Twitter or at conferences).

For approximately six weeks, you meet for a one-hour video call where you reflect on a weekly article or video clip. Each week has a different facilitator who shares on one challenge he or she is facing, then the other members of the group offer feedback and ideas. The following week, that person reports on how the suggestions worked out in practice, and then the next person takes his or her place as facilitator. Mastermind groups are a great way to hear and apply new perspectives when considering a topic. Here, no one is the single expert, and all can contribute through inquiry and exploration of fresh ideas.

Think Tanks

Traditionally organized in research institutes, government agencies, nonprofits, or high-tech spaces, think tanks bring together great minds on subjects for intensive thinking and planning. Through the creation of an education think tank program, ideas can be shared, molded, extended, and activated. Think tanks in schools can be likened to a Professional Learning Community (PLC) that is electrified.

To organize an education think tank in your school or district (or maybe even virtually), get your topic, get your people, and get a plan. Perhaps you want to examine digital equity with art educators for four weeks. Or maybe you want

Read with Audrey

Thinking back, I am not sure how I discovered **Read with Audrey** (readwithaudrey .com), but from the first moment of hearing how it worked, I was hooked. Read with Audrey, or simply Audrey, creates meaningful online experiences that encourage conversation and connection. Audrey is a peer-driven community that matches pairs of individuals, who read thoughtfully chosen books aloud together, sparking interesting conversations and creating meaningful relationships. Audrey is for anyone who enjoys reading, would like to develop a sense of connectedness with others, and values diverse points of view. All around the world, every week, people in the Audrey community are reading aloud to each other.

When I joined Audrey, I was paired with Sofia, a photojournalist in Rio de Janeiro. After being connected by email, we decided to meet virtually on Mondays. Week to week, we would take turns reading a chapter to each other during our thirty- to forty-five-minute calls. After the reading, we would reflect, sharing connections of the characters to our own lives; I shared on my children and husband and travels for work, she shared on her photo assignments, on the political climate in her country, and on her mother in Portugal who like me had been a teacher of children with special needs.

to conduct a six-week think tank that will take action on bringing diverse books into middle school social studies classes. Think tanks can provide a powerful, solution-focused experience for educators anytime, anywhere, and on any topic that needs brainpower applied to it.

Edcamps

With Edcamps, learning is participant-driven, as sessions for the day are determined organically with teachers themselves indicating topics they want to learn and share. Learning is centered on passions and questions relevant to the lives of attendees and their learning communities, so no two Edcamps are

We thought deeply about our book *The Language of Kindness*, a story of a critical care nurse in London. We connected on Instagram, introduced each other to friends with shared interests, and looked forward to our next book *The Wind in My Hair: My Fight for Freedom in Modern Iran*. As English was not Sofia's first language, she shared that she had been a little nervous at first reading aloud to me, particularly because there were medical terms in the book that she had not seen before. Our weekly readings, giving us moments of pause from hurried days, were special and treasured. Both busy and short on time, we found a way to make time because it mattered.

If you are interested in trying out Audrey, the journey begins by completing an introductory profile. It takes approximately five minutes. The Audrey "community connectors" use the introductory profiles to match people with a reading partner—often someone with shared interests but a different life journey.

The "community connectors" introduce the reader and listener to one another (you can choose to be a reader, a listener, or both) and share the book free of charge. Readers decide on a time to meet in a Reading Room, and then the story begins.

To consider: Using Read with Audrey as a model, how might you connect your students with children from around the world in oral storytelling experiences?

alike. Edcamps are free and open to all educators worldwide, and Edcamp-style PD can be incorporated into faculty meetings or district-wide events. To learn more about Edcamps, visit edcamp.org.

EDUCATION MOVEMENTS TO PROMPT ACTION

New trends in global PD not only provide purpose, motivation, new knowledge, and skills, they also afford educators autonomy and agency to revolutionize the landscape of education and positively change the way educators access and share information for professional growth. Described below are three hashtags that have prompted movements and action in education.

#oneword

Each January, motivated and resolute teachers ready to take on the new year commit to their intentions and goals with the #oneword challenge. After selecting one representative word as a guide for action, teachers share messages using blog posts or digital images created with tools such as Adobe Spark or Canva. The messages are sent with excitement to a PLN full of accountability partners. Check out #oneword on social media and feel free to jump in anytime with your own one word.

#100challenge

The #100challenge creatively brings together social media, the arts, and teacher well-being—all around professional learning. Committed to extending knowledge of global topics in education and overall personal happiness, participating teachers watch a TED Talk of their choice each day and then document learning in the form of a sketchnote. These visual representations of concepts are then shared on social media platforms. Check it out by searching #100challenge on Twitter, Instagram, or Facebook.

#CelebrateMonday

To bring positivity to Mondays, principal Sean Gaillard (@smgaillard) set out to give the first day of each school week a needed boost. Starting with one tweet of a #CelebrateMonday hashtag, Sean launched a global movement of educators who share messages of good news on Mondays. Teachers share photos, inspirational quotes, celebratory videos, and more, all joining to change mindsets and build excitement for learning. Join Sean and the thousands of teachers emphasizing the positive on social media every Monday with the hashtag #CelebrateMonday.

STUDY TRIPS

New technologies of the digital age allow educators to cross school walls and national borders to develop professional learning networks around the world. Teachers who value working on global projects are recognizing the extraordinary power of collaborative travel experiences. By joining global study trips, teams of educators can travel to examine problems of global significance, explore new cultures or educational practices, or attend professional summits, conferences, or consortiums.

MICHAEL HERNANDEZ

6.3 Michael Hernandez leads study trips, like this one to Guatemala.

Advanced tech tools enable learning teams not only to plan trips, but also to work together during all stages of travel to share and communicate. Michael Hernandez (@cinehead), a high school teacher and media literacy expert, hosts annual digital storytelling study trips for educators. (He also organizes trips for students.) Here he shares on a recent study trip to Guatemala:

Digital storytelling—communicating ideas and sharing knowledge—is a vital skill for our students to be successful, but most teachers have no formal training in it and don't know how to integrate it into their classrooms. Helping teachers learn digital storytelling and how to teach it has become my niche.

I've presented on the topic at many conferences and PD trainings, but I feel that the best way to learn is to have an immersive experience, to learn and practice over time. We started offering teacher-centered digital storytelling trips that model a student experience, where you travel to a developing country to learn about digital storytelling, and also to learn about the people, culture, and history of that country. It's a project with purpose. The learning of history is embedded in the project, and vice versa. I really think that the only way any kind of learning is going to stick is if you care about what you're doing and you can see the purpose behind what you're learning. When participants become invested in the topic, like on these trips, there is passion and purpose, and the learning becomes invisible. You don't realize you're learning technical skills or history, because you're so invested in the topic and project.

When I travelled with several teachers to Guatemala to teach them how to make documentaries, we encountered a particularly heart-wrenching obstacle. One of the teachers was interviewing a young woman who was about fourteen years old and happened to ask her what she does for fun in her free time. Our guide explained to us that this was a sensitive subject for the teenager, because she didn't have free time like American kids. Her family couldn't afford the $40 it cost for school supplies, so she wasn't able to attend school that year, and instead had to work in the family business. Since she wasn't around her friends who were in school, she didn't have much of a social life.

This was a stunning surprise for us, since we never considered our own cultural bias and the role that economics plays in the most basic routines of life that we take for granted. We project our own lifestyle and privilege onto others, assuming that they have what we do. Through this experience, we all learned one of the most important lessons: our cultural blind spots put us in a place where we were unable to see the real story of economics and politics in other cultures.

Michael shares on media literacy, storytelling, and teaching on his website, social channels, blog, newsletter, and podcast. Be sure to check in with him at michael-hernandez.net.

ISTE OPPORTUNITIES FOR CONNECTING, LEARNING, AND SHARING

ISTE offers many opportunities for educators to continue their professional development. Educators can connect year-round through more than twenty Professional Learning Networks in subject areas such as digital equity, learning spaces, and teacher education. ISTE U is a set of curated professional learning experiences, and ISTE Books offers more than eighty titles that focus on critical topics in edtech. Information on all of ISTE's offerings is available at iste.org.

TAKE ACTION
CREATE YOUR PERSONALIZED LEARNING PLAN

If you could design the ultimate PD experience for yourself, what would it look like? How would that type of learning make you feel? Through a backward design process, create your proposed personalized learning plan and then share it (with a colleague, with an administrator, with a friend). Here are guiding questions to answer as you prepare your plan:

QUESTION 1: What is a topic or area within education that you would like to study or know more about?

QUESTION 2: What skills could you develop in your study of that topic?

QUESTION 3: Who would benefit from your new learning?

QUESTION 4: What types of activities would help you to achieve this new knowledge or set of skills?

QUESTION 5: Following research, what are the specific activities or experiences you would like to participate in for your personalized PD plan?

QUESTION 6: Who would be interested in hearing about your idea? Now is your chance to share! (Teach boldly, right?)

BOLD INVITATION
INTERNATIONAL CONFERENCES THAT PRIORITIZE SOCIAL GOOD AND GLOBAL ACTION

Many conferences and in-person events bring educators together to explore topics of social good, equity in education, social action, and the use of edtech and innovation. As you work to teach boldly to transform learning, find an international conference that prioritizes social good and global action and that offers a different perspective on education from what you are accustomed to. Here are a handful of my favorites:

- **LEARNING BY DESIGN.** February in Brussels, Belgium; presented by International School of Brussels.

- **SXSW EDU.** March in Austin, Texas; presented by SXSW.

- **ISTE CONFERENCE AND EXPO.** June in various locations; presented by the International Society for Technology in Education (ISTE).

- **SOCIAL GOOD SUMMIT.** September in New York City, New York; presented by Mashable and UN Foundation.

- **SHIFTINEDU.** October in Miami, Florida; presented by St. Stephen's School.

- **UNLEASH.** November in various locations; presented by UNLEASH Organization.

MY PEACEMAKER PROFILE ACTIVITY #6
MY PEACEMAKER VISION STATEMENT

As we come to the conclusion of our *My PeaceMAKER Profile* journey, now can be a time for reflection. Consider the thoughts you had around ways to best use your time to align with the things you value. Reflect on the "goosebumps moments" that came from your conversations with your students about their interests, their hopes, the connections to the classroom space and to the world around us all.

Bring all your work and ideas and hopes and dreams together to consider how you would complete the sentence "I'd like to teach the world to _____." When you are set with your response, print out this sign (**Figure 6.4** and available on jenwilliamsedu.com/peacemaker-profile.html) and add the words that represent your purpose as a teacher. Consider sharing on social media with the hashtags #TeachBoldly and #PeaceMAKER and please be sure to tag me, @JenWilliamsEdu!

I'd like to teach the world to _____ .
#TeachBoldly
#PeaceMAKER

6.4 Print out this sign and add the words that represent your purpose as a teacher.

Intersection of Technology, Pedagogy, and Peace

Koen Timmers, Belgian professor, Global Teacher Prize finalist, TeachSDGs Founding Ambassador
Kakuma Project, Climate Action Project, Innovation Lab Schools with Jane Goodall
Twitter: @zelfstudie

When I was that young girl I described at the start of this book, the one who was eager to learn anything and everything about Africa, one of my childhood heroes was Jane Goodall, a female scientist who boldly entered an area of science that had not been explored or really even considered. Thinking of wild chimpanzees as having emotions and communications systems, science with empathy for the greater good of all was my jam! I never would have thought that my path would ever intersect with Dr. Goodall's.

But one day it did.

In 2018, my friend and education hero, Koen Timmers (@zelfstudie), contacted me about work he was doing in refugee camps in Africa. Needing an instructional designer and knowing my commitment to the Global Goals and to quality education for all, he wanted to see if I would volunteer with him on a project he was doing with Jane Goodall. (He didn't know then that my dog was named Fig after Goodall's chimpanzee, Figan.) I absolutely was in for the work!

Koen had been leading the Climate Action Project, involving 515 schools across eighty-five countries—all taking action for climate change. When he contacted me in 2018, he was looking for teachers willing to donate time to teach lessons through Skype to children in the Kakuma refugee camp, which shelters 200,000 refugees fleeing war and hunger in Sudan, Burundi, Somalia, Congo, and other places.

That year, 1,500 young children had arrived at the refugee camp without families. The camp had no resources, Wi-Fi, or even a laptop computer, but Koen worked to find a way. He sent his own laptop.

He soon realized that the camp lacked a power supply, so in partnership with the UN Refugee Agency and the Lutheran World Federation, he worked to invent and supply solar suitcases. "The Skype lessons were an instant success," says Koen. "Imagine a classroom housing 200 students taking a look at one small laptop screen (projectkakuma.com). I taught math, science, English, and religion. But in fact we did more. We discussed hobbies, had good laughs about sports, discussed culture, and had fun."

Over 300 teachers have joined to do three Skype lessons per week. Some teachers have traveled to the camp to train people there to teach, while others have sent books and STEM robot kits. "Education is the only way out, as the refugees are locked in the camp. And the future looks bright." Koen says.

We are now building Innovation Lab School programs across the world to use technology to teach and change lives (innovationsdglab.com). Our Global Goals Book curriculum, authored by an international team of educators, incorporates design thinking and the creation of an advocacy film around the SDGs; it is available for free through Creative Commons.

With the help of Jane Goodall, the Jane Goodall Institute, and a growing list of partners and supporters, we are on a mission to bring free, quality education to every child, everywhere. We are hopeful that all children who are dreaming of living in a safe, happy, and peaceful world can have those dreams come true.

FINAL THOUGHTS
FOR PEOPLE AND PLANET

This book is offered as an invitation to go fearlessly into the future. We are entering a new time in which we will interact regularly with technologies such as artificial intelligence and machine learning, and it will be imperative that our humanity is preserved. Decisions will need to be made based on empathy and compassion with humans at the center. What we are learning and teaching today can quickly become obsolete, so we need to be comfortable with change and prepared to be not only lifelong learners but also lifewide learners.

When we see that 90% of all children in developing countries are enrolled in school, we need to remember that this means that tens of millions of students globally still remain out of school.

How might we ensure quality education and accessible and equitable learning for all?

Our future, without question, is determined by what happens in our schools today. As we take action on social good—as peacekeepers and peaceMAKERS, with and for our students—we can work together for the good of people and planet. Be kind, be curious, be bold.

Excited to hear where your journey takes you!

In solidarity with you,

Jen

ISTE STANDARDS FOR EDUCATORS

The ISTE Standards for Educators are your road map to helping students become empowered learners. These standards will deepen your practice, promote collaboration with peers, challenge you to rethink traditional approaches and prepare students to drive their own learning.

Empowered Professional

1. **Learner**

   Educators continually improve their practice by learning from and with others and exploring proven and promising practices that leverage technology to improve student learning. Educators:

   a. Set professional learning goals to explore and apply pedagogical approaches made possible by technology and reflect on their effectiveness.

   b. Pursue professional interests by creating and actively participating in local and global learning networks.

   c. Stay current with research that supports improved student learning outcomes, including findings from the learning sciences.

2. **Leader**

   Educators seek out opportunities for leadership to support student empowerment and success and to improve teaching and learning. Educators:

   a. Shape, advance and accelerate a shared vision for empowered learning with technology by engaging with education stakeholders.

   b. Advocate for equitable access to educational technology, digital content and learning opportunities to meet the diverse needs of all students.

   c. Model for colleagues the identification, exploration, evaluation, curation and adoption of new digital resources and tools for learning.

3. Citizen

Educators inspire students to positively contribute to and responsibly participate in the digital world. Educators:

   a. Create experiences for learners to make positive, socially responsible contributions and exhibit empathetic behavior online that build relationships and community.

   b. Establish a learning culture that promotes curiosity and critical examination of online resources and fosters digital literacy and media fluency.

   c. Mentor students in safe, legal and ethical practices with digital tools and the protection of intellectual rights and property.

   d. Model and promote management of personal data and digital identity and protect student data privacy.

Learning Catalyst

1. Collaborator

Educators dedicate time to collaborate with both colleagues and students to improve practice, discover and share resources and ideas, and solve problems. Educators:

   a. Dedicate planning time to collaborate with colleagues to create authentic learning experiences that leverage technology.

   b. Collaborate and co-learn with students to discover and use new digital resources and diagnose and troubleshoot technology issues.

   c. Use collaborative tools to expand students' authentic, real-world learning experiences by engaging virtually with experts, teams and students, locally and globally.

   d. Demonstrate cultural competency when communicating with students, parents and colleagues and interact with them as co-collaborators in student learning.

2. Designer

   Educators design authentic, learner-driven activities and environments that recognize and accommodate learner variability. Educators:

   a. Use technology to create, adapt and personalize learning experiences that foster independent learning and accommodate learner differences and needs.

   b. Design authentic learning activities that align with content area standards and use digital tools and resources to maximize active, deep learning.

   c. Explore and apply instructional design principles to create innovative digital learning environments that engage and support learning.

3. Facilitator

   Educators facilitate learning with technology to support student achievement of the 2016 ISTE Standards for Students. Educators:

   a. Foster a culture where students take ownership of their learning goals and outcomes in both independent and group settings.

   b. Manage the use of technology and student learning strategies in digital platforms, virtual environments, hands-on makerspaces or in the field.

   c. Create learning opportunities that challenge students to use a design process and computational thinking to innovate and solve problems.

    d. Model and nurture creativity and creative expression to communicate ideas, knowledge or connections.

4. Analyst

Educators understand and use data to drive their instruction and support students in achieving their learning goals. Educators:

    a. Provide alternative ways for students to demonstrate competency and reflect on their learning using technology.

    b. Use technology to design and implement a variety of formative and summative assessments that accommodate learner needs, provide timely feedback to students and inform instruction.

    c. Use assessment data to guide progress and communicate with students, parents and education stakeholders to build student self-direction.

ISTE STANDARDS FOR STUDENTS

The 2016 ISTE Standards for Students emphasize the skills and qualities we want for students, enabling them to engage and thrive in a connected, digital world. The standards are designed for use by educators across the curriculum, with every age student, with a goal of cultivating these skills throughout a student's academic career. Both students and teachers will be responsible for achieving foundational technology skills to fully apply the standards. The reward, however, will be educators who skillfully mentor and inspire students to amplify learning with technology and challenge them to be agents of their own learning.

1. Empowered Learner

   Students leverage technology to take an active role in choosing, achieving and demonstrating competency in their learning goals, informed by the learning sciences. Students:

   a. articulate and set personal learning goals, develop strategies leveraging technology to achieve them and reflect on the learning process itself to improve learning outcomes.

   b. build networks and customize their learning environments in ways that support the learning process.

   c. use technology to seek feedback that informs and improves their practice and to demonstrate their learning in a variety of ways.

   d. understand the fundamental concepts of technology operations, demonstrate the ability to choose, use and troubleshoot current technologies and are able to transfer their knowledge to explore emerging technologies.

2. Digital Citizen

Students recognize the rights, responsibilities and opportunities of living, learning and working in an interconnected digital world, and they act and model in ways that are safe, legal and ethical. Students:

a. cultivate and manage their digital identity and reputation and are aware of the permanence of their actions in the digital world.

b. engage in positive, safe, legal and ethical behavior when using technology, including social interactions online or when using networked devices.

c. demonstrate an understanding of and respect for the rights and obligations of using and sharing intellectual property.

d. manage their personal data to maintain digital privacy and security and are aware of data-collection technology used to track their navigation online.

3. Knowledge Constructor

Students critically curate a variety of resources using digital tools to construct knowledge, produce creative artifacts and make meaningful learning experiences for themselves and others. Students:

a. plan and employ effective research strategies to locate information and other resources for their intellectual or creative pursuits.

b. evaluate the accuracy, perspective, credibility and relevance of information, media, data or other resources.

c. curate information from digital resources using a variety of tools and methods to create collections of artifacts that demonstrate meaningful connections or conclusions.

d. build knowledge by actively exploring real-world issues and problems, developing ideas and theories and pursuing answers and solutions.

4. Innovative Designer

Students use a variety of technologies within a design process to identify and solve problems by creating new, useful or imaginative solutions. Students:

a. know and use a deliberate design process for generating ideas, testing theories, creating innovative artifacts or solving authentic problems.

b. select and use digital tools to plan and manage a design process that considers design constraints and calculated risks.

c. develop, test and refine prototypes as part of a cyclical design process.

d. exhibit a tolerance for ambiguity, perseverance and the capacity to work with open-ended problems.

5. Computational Thinker

Students develop and employ strategies for understanding and solving problems in ways that leverage the power of technological methods to develop and test solutions. Students:

a. formulate problem definitions suited for technology-assisted methods such as data analysis, abstract models and algorithmic thinking in exploring and finding solutions.

b. collect data or identify relevant data sets, use digital tools to analyze them, and represent data in various ways to facilitate problem-solving and decision-making.

c. break problems into component parts, extract key information, and develop descriptive models to understand complex systems or facilitate problem-solving.

d. understand how automation works and use algorithmic thinking to develop a sequence of steps to create and test automated solutions.

6. Creative Communicator

Students communicate clearly and express themselves creatively for a variety of purposes using the platforms, tools, styles, formats and digital media appropriate to their goals. Students:

   a. choose the appropriate platforms and tools for meeting the desired objectives of their creation or communication.

   b. create original works or responsibly repurpose or remix digital resources into new creations.

   c. communicate complex ideas clearly and effectively by creating or using a variety of digital objects such as visualizations, models or simulations.

   d. publish or present content that customizes the message and medium for their intended audiences.

7. Global Collaborator

Students use digital tools to broaden their perspectives and enrich their learning by collaborating with others and working effectively in teams locally and globally. Students:

   a. use digital tools to connect with learners from a variety of backgrounds and cultures, engaging with them in ways that broaden mutual understanding and learning.

   b. use collaborative technologies to work with others, including peers, experts or community members, to examine issues and problems from multiple viewpoints.

   c. contribute constructively to project teams, assuming various roles and responsibilities to work effectively toward a common goal.

   d. explore local and global issues and use collaborative technologies to work with others to investigate solutions.

APPENDIX C
THREE PURPOSE-DRIVEN EDTECH PROGRAMS

WORLD'S LARGEST LESSON

worldslargestlesson.globalgoals.org
@TheWorldsLesson on Twitter

The World's Largest Lesson (WLL) is an educational initiative run in partnership with UNICEF to ensure all children everywhere feel inspired to take action for the UN Sustainable Development Goals. Each year in September, the team at WLL releases a lesson—*The World's Largest Lesson*—that teachers from all around the world can access for free online at worldslargestlesson.globalgoals.org. The *World's Largest Lesson* feels big (and *is* big), but the lesson is made locally relevant by asking teachers and students to use their own environment as inspiration for their learning. The content is action-focused, asking students to consider ways they can change or take action on the goals in their local communities.

"We aim to inspire young people into continually asking questions, being curious and open to thinking about what ways they can make the most meaningful impact," says WLL's director, Alison Bellwood. She shared this story with me:

WORLD'S LARGEST LESSON

> *One particular story that has stuck with us is one that happened in Jordan in early 2018. A group of students had been learning about the Goals, when they came across a news article about a widow in their local community who was unable to provide food for her young family. She was almost destitute. The students decided to help her by raising money through a charity raffle at school. But they then went a step further and thought how they could help this woman in a way that empowered her as well as helped her to provide for her family. After speaking with the woman, they decided to use the money they had raised to buy her two goats. Their reasoning behind this was that the woman could look after the goats and make money from their milk, and therefore be able to provide for her family. That level of empathy and thoughtfulness shown from the students has really stuck with me. Our biggest hope for the future is that all children everywhere know about the Goals and take action for them—so that there can be millions more stories like the goat story!*

Many familiar people have written content and advocated for World's Largest Lesson, including Malala Yousafzai, Sir Ken Robinson, and Emma Watson, and since starting in September of 2015, the World's Largest Lesson has reached millions of students in more than 130 countries. A good way to start using WLL with your students is to watch the animations (worldslargestlesson.global-goals.org/animated-films) that explain and break down the Goals. The videos identify a process of change-making for students to create their own purpose-driven projects for their local communities.

TeachSDGs and World's Largest Lesson work together to connect teachers and students to the Global Goals. Please share on social media with #GlobalGoals, #WorldsLargestLesson, and #TeachSDGs.

WORLD'S LARGEST LESSON

EMPATICO

Empatico.

empatico.org
@EmpaticoOrg on Twitter

Empatico is an edtech nonprofit organization expanding past the traditional boundaries of learning by combining the best in technology with the best of humanity. In their mission to spread kindness and spark empathy around the world through virtual exchange, they are set to connect one million students age six through eleven by the year 2020.

Students participate in an Empatico virtual exchange.

Incubated with funding from The KIND Foundation, Empatico was created to build understanding across lines of difference and to deepen relationships regardless of location. As the son of a Holocaust survivor, founder Daniel Lubetsky understands the importance and power of recognizing our shared humanity. Looking to create an "empathy revolution," the team at Empatico is focused on strengthening social-emotional learning (specifically cognitive empathy) by providing activities that help students learn and practice essential skills of perspective taking, critical thinking, cooperation, and respectful communication.

Empatico aims to provide opportunities for educators to connect their elementary classrooms with others around the world through a combination of live video and standards-based activities. Why this age group? "At Empatico, we focus on students of ages 6—11 because children at this age are old enough to understand their role in the world, but young enough to be positively influenced by experiences," says Noah Garcia-Hassell of Empatico. "By creating shared and engaging interactions for educators and students, we believe we can spark a global movement to spread kindness and empathy throughout the world."

Aligned with their mission to meaningfully partner with educators, Empatico directly uses teacher and student feedback in the product design. Continues Garcia-Hassell:

> We have collaborated with education partners to create a tool that makes it easier than ever to bring virtual connections to their classrooms in an intentional and powerful way. Through a robust combination of research, surveys, interviews, pilot studies, classroom observations, and open conversation with the educator community, our team is continuously collecting and incorporating feedback based on classroom needs voiced by teachers. Our goal is to work closely with educators through every step of the design process in order to provide a product that seamlessly fits into their classrooms (both in terms of tech requirements and curricular alignment) with as much ease and flexibility as possible.

Empatico is free and available to any educator (including classroom teachers, media specialists, guidance counselors, art/music teachers, and administrators) who works directly with students ages six through eleven, has internet access, and has access to a device with a camera. After creating an empatico.org teacher account, classrooms are matched with a partner class and then are guided through the process of preparation and live video virtual exchange.

Here are the steps for teachers who are ready to get started:

1. Create a free teacher account at empatico.org. Elementary educators anywhere in the world can sign up.

2. Share times in a typical week when your class is available to connect over live video.

3. Select from nine standards- and research-based activities that align to your lessons or areas of interest:

   - Get to Know You
   - Our Local Landmarks
   - Everyday Energy
   - Folktales to Learn From

- Festivals around the World
- Ways We Play
- Helping Hands
- Weather Out the Window
- Community Cartographers

4. Watch for a message containing information on your matched classroom.

5. Prepare with your matched classroom teacher and your students using the provided resources.

6. Join for videoconferencing on the empatico.org site and interact with your new global friends.

7. Gather your students to reflect on the experience in a Reflection Circle activity.

For more information on Empatico or to connect with the team, visit empatico.org.

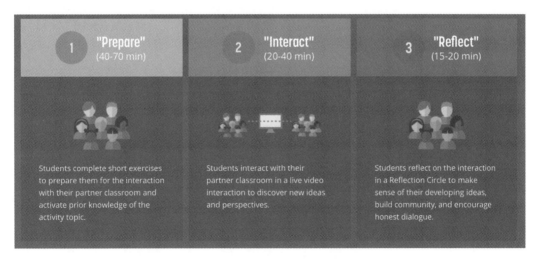

Empatico virtual exchange interactions progress through three stages.

ROCK YOUR WORLD

Inspiring students to change their world

rock-your-world.org
@RockYourWorld70 on Twitter

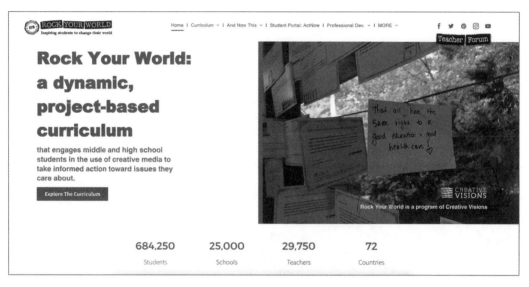

Rock-Your-World.org offers an online human rights curriculum for middle and high school students.

Rock Your World (RYW), a program of Creative Visions, inspires young people to use the power of photographs, words, film, paint, ink, dance, and music to draw attention to human rights issues. Rock Your World offers a free online curriculum for educators of middle and high school students and provides students with opportunities to research real-world issues anchored in the Universal Declaration of Human Rights. Once students have identified issues about which they feel passionate, they are provided with tools to create a dynamic, multimedia advocacy campaign.

Founded by Kathy Eldon and her daughter Amy Eldon Turtletaub in 1997, Creative Visions honors the legacy of Dan Eldon, Kathy's son and Amy's brother, by supporting and empowering creative activists worldwide. Dan Eldon was an adventurous, artistic, and altruistic young man. Growing up in Kenya, he developed his artistic talents by keeping detailed and illustrative multimedia journals and by challenging himself as a photographer. He also led student aid expeditions and creative campaigns for those he knew were in need. The youngest photojournalist hired by Reuters, Dan Eldon was a respected war photographer and was covering the conflict in Somalia at the time of his violent death at the age of twenty-two.

Rock Your World invites dialogue around human rights and responsibilities in education.

The team at Rock Your World believes students are the changemakers of today, and RYW is committed to making space in our classrooms to honor our students and what they are capable of accomplishing. Following a project-based learning (PBL) model, RYW creates pathways for students to engage in authentic, real-world learning and calls on teachers to introduce a changemaking curriculum that reflects the urgency of today's current events. "Students demand relevant learning, and we are obligated to provide it to them," say Jessica Burnquist and Tricia Baldes of RYW. "When human rights are at the center of curricular content, students will engage in their learning in a personal way that will manifest in better communities, countries, and the world."

RYW allows teachers to bring human rights and social justice to the top of the learning hierarchy. Through the free online curriculum, students are guided to create their human rights advocacy campaigns with choice in method of expression: make a film, write a song, or write persuasively.

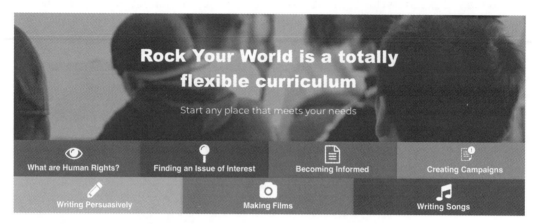

The lessons in Rock Your World's free online curriculum progress through a series of steps, but students can start wherever suits them best.

RYW meets you and your students where you are with an enter-where-you-wish curricular design. Lessons and resources help students to (1) understand human rights, (2) find an issue of interest, (3) become informed, and (4) create and publish a campaign. Completed digital artifacts can then be uploaded for peer review and feedback.

The skills involved include critical and creative thinking, the ability to contextualize a human rights issue for the purposes of drawing awareness and proposing solutions, and utilizing the arts to convey areas of an issue that students want to make known for their audience.

- **INQUIRY:** developing questions to drive research and response throughout the process

- **READING AND RESEARCH:** self-directed reading and research to answer inquiry-based questions through the process of the campaign creation

- **COLLABORATION:** working with partners and in groups to develop creative responses to human rights issues

- **PROBLEM-SOLVING** (large and small scale):

  - looking at human rights issues in the world and proposing possible responses and solutions

  - looking at the creative action in process, identifying possible problems and proposing solutions

- **COMMUNICATION:** Using various modes of communication (writing, speaking, art) fused with technology to convey a message selected for a targeted audience

- **COMPETENCIES OF SOCIAL-EMOTIONAL LEARNING, RISK TAKING, AND REFLECTION**

Sample campaigns might include:

- Climate change

- Immigration

- Access to health and education

- Freedom of expression

- Women and children's rights

- Hunger, homelessness, and poverty

To learn more about Rock Your World, visit rock-your-world.org. Professional development workshops for educators are available by request and are ongoing at the Museum of Tolerance in Los Angeles. Watch for Rock Your World International in Mexico City, Kenya, Tanzania, France, and England.

APPENDIX D
SCHOOLWIDE LEARNING EXPERIENCE

Schools and networks of educators can engage with *Teach Boldly* and the My PeaceMAKER Profile experience as groups.

Ideas for school groups, Professional Learning Communities (PLCs), and online Professional Learning Networks (PLNs) include:

- **BOOK CLUBS:** In person and online

- **TWITTER CHATS:** Thirty- to sixty-minute online conversations using the hashtag #TeachBoldly

- **GROUP READINGS OF CHAPTERS**

- **GROUP COLLABORATION ON MY PEACEMAKER PROFILE ACTIVITIES**

More ideas for groups are available at jenwilliamsedu.com/teach-boldly-schools.

REFERENCES

Asia Society, & OECD (2018). *Teaching for global competence in a rapidly changing world.* http://dx.doi.org/10.1787/9789264289024-en Retrieved from: https://asiasociety.org /education/teaching-global-competence-rapidly-changing-world

B Lab (2018). Certified B-corporation. Retrieved from https://bcorporation.net

Baldes, T., & Burnquist, J. (2018, December). Personal interview.

Bellwood, A. (2018, December). Personal interview.

Benjamin, J. (2018, December). Personal interview.

Buckley, D. (2019, January). Personal interview.

Bugaj, S. V. (2013). *Pixar's 22 rules of story (that aren't really Pixar's): Analyzed.* eBook. Retrieved from: static1.squarespace.com/static/52675998e4b07faca3f636a5/t/527f0a75e4b012bf9 e7361c5/1384057461885/Pixar22RulesAnalyzed_Bugaj.pdf

Burns, M. (2018, December). Personal interview.

Burns, M., & Forta, B. (2018). *40 ways to inject creativity into your classroom with Adobe Spark.* Irvine, CA: EdtechTeam Press.

Christensen, K., et al. (2009). Ageing populations: The challenges ahead. *The Lancet, 374*(9696), 1196-1208. doi.org/10.1016/S0140-6736(09)61460-4

Church, E. (2018, December). Personal interview.

Coats, E. (2011). Tweets. Retrieved from: https://twitter.com/lawnrocket

Collins, M. (2018, December). Personal interview.

Cooley, M. (1980). *Architect or bee? The human price of technology.* London, England: The Hogarth Press.

EEOC. (2018). *Diversity in high tech.* Retrieved from: https://www.eeoc.gov/eeoc/statistics /reports/hightech/

Fleming, L. (2019, March). Personal interview.

Fleming, L. (2018). *The kickstart guide to making GREAT makerspaces*. Thousand Oaks: CA: Corwin.

Fleming, L. (2015). *World of making: Best practices for establishing a makerspace for your school*. Thousand Oaks, CA: Corwin.

Garcia-Hassell, N. (2018, December). Personal interview.

Google. (2018). Google diversity annual report. Retrieved from: https://diversity.google /annual-report/

Google. (2017). Making progress on diversity and inclusion. Retrieved from: https://blog.google /outreach-initiatives/diversity/making-progress-diversity-and-inclusion/

Helliwell, J., Layard, R., & Sachs, J. (2019). *World happiness report 2019*. New York: United Nations Sustainable Development Solutions Network. Retrieved from: http://worldhappiness .report/ed/2019/

Hernandez, M. (2018, December). Personal interview.

IDEO. (2015). *The field guide to human-centered design*. Canada: IDEO.

International Literacy Association. (2018). Literacy glossary. Retrieved from: https://www .literacyworldwide.org/get-resources/literacy-glossary

International Organization for Standardization. (2009). *Ergonomics of human system interaction—Part 210: Human-centered design for interactive systems*. Retrieved from: http://www.iso.org/standard/52075.html

International Society for Technology in Education (ISTE). (2019). ISTE Standards. Retrieved from: https://www.iste.org/standards

Khan, S. (2013). *The one world schoolhouse: Education reimagined*. New York, NY: Twelve.

Knowles, M. S. (1970). *The modern practice of adult education: Andragogy versus pedagogy*. New York: Association Press.

Kurani, D. (2018). Google Code Next lab. Retrieved from: https://kurani.us/ google-code-next-lab/

Kurani, D. (2018, December). Personal interview.

Lee, A. (2013, November). Welcome to the unicorn club: Learning from billion-dollar startups. *TechCrunch*. Retrieved from: techcrunch.com/2013/11/02/welcome-to-the-unicorn-club/

Marcinek, A. (2018, December). Personal interview.

McKim, A. (2018, December). Personal interview.

McNair, A. (2017). *Genius hour: Passion projects that ignite innovation and student inquiry.* Waco, TX: Prufrock Press.

Mor Barak, M. (2018). The practice and science of social good: Next generation paths for social change. *Research on Social Work Practice, 28*(6), 762.

National Council of Nonprofits. (2018). What is a "nonprofit?" Retrieved from: councilofnonprofits.org

OECD. (2018). *Education at a glance 2018: OECD indicators.* Paris, France: OECD Publishing. Retrieved from: https://doi.org/10.1787/eag-2018-en.

Ohno, T. (1988). *Toyota production system: Beyond large-scale production.* Portland, OR: Productivity, Inc.

Peters, S. (2018, December). Personal interview.

Santa Clara County Office of Education. (2016). My Name, My Identity. Retrieved from: https://www.mynamemyidentity.org

Thompson, D. (2017, November). Google X and the science of radical creativity. *The Atlantic.* Retrieved from: https://www.theatlantic.com/magazine/archive/2017/11 /x-google-moonshot-factory/540648/

Timmers, K. (2018, December). Personal interview.

United States Bureau of Labor Statistics. (2019). Retrieved from: https://www.bls.gov/home.htm

United States Department of Education. (2017). *Reimagining the role of technology in education: 2017 National Education Technology Plan update.* Washington, DC: Office of Education Technology.

Van Ledtje, O. (2019, March). Personal interview.

Vodafone. (2018). *Girls and mobile.* Retrieved from: https://www.vodafone.com/content /foundation/girlsandmobile.html

Ultanir, E. (2012). An epistemological glance at the constructivist approach: Constructivist learning in Dewey, Piaget, and Montessori. *International Journal of Instruction, 5*(2), 195—212.

Vygotsky, L. S. (1978). *Mind in society.* Cambridge, MA: Harvard University Press.

INDEX

YOUR OPINION MATTERS:
TELL US HOW WE'RE DOING!

Your feedback helps ISTE create the best possible resources for teaching and learning in the digital age. Share your thoughts with the community or tell us how we're doing!

You can:

- Write a review at amazon.com or barnesandnoble.com.

- Mention this book on social media and follow ISTE on Twitter @iste, Facebook @ISTEconnects or Instagram @isteconnects.

- Email us at books@iste.org with your questions or comments.